A German Bohemian Immigration

The Population Shift from Western Bohemia to Calumet County, Wisconsin

Joan Naomi Steiner, PhD

SCENERY HEIGHTS
Publishing

Neenah, Wisconsin (USA)

A German Bohemian Immigration

The Population Shift from Western Bohemia to Calumet County, Wisconsin

Second Edition

Front cover images: Top photo shows the author's great-great-grandfather, Adalbert Steiner (Steiner family collection); Bottom photo shows (from left) the St. Charles Rectory, Church and School in Calumet County, Wisconsin, 1908 (Postcard collection, privately held by Herb Buhl, Chilton, Wisconsin.)

Back cover image: Aerial view of St. Charles Church in Charlesburg, Calumet County, Wisconsin, prior to 1950 (Picture collection, privately held by Herb Buhl, Chilton, Wisconsin.)

ISBN: 979-8-9865709-0-7

Scenery Heights Publications
Neenah, Wisconsin (USA)

Dedication

To my granddaughter, Madeline

A shaper of dreams

Contents

Part I
Research

This monument marks the final resting place in St. Charles Cemetery (Calumet County, Wisconsin) for Adalbert Steiner, the author's great-great-grandfather and genesis of her research. (Photo courtesy of the Herb Buhl Collection)

Introduction

Hundreds of German Bohemians from western Bohemia immigrated to the Town of Brothertown in Calumet County, Wisconsin, beginning in the 1850s. This book in many ways is their untold story.

Background

Chilton is Calumet County's seat of government and has been since 1853.[1] It was a village in the 1860s. The only media outlet at the time was the local weekly newspaper, *The Chilton Times*, which was established in 1857.[2] The *Times* reported on area events, politics, and the lives of those living in the community. Past issues of the *Times* are historical snapshots of community life covering more than 160 years.

---

[1] *Calumet County, Wisconsin Genealogy & History* (http://freepages.genealogy.rootsweb.com/~sheboygan/_ : accessed 10 March 2022), "Chilton."

[2] *Calumet County, Wisconsin Genealogy & History,* "Chilton."

We begin with a news article published by *The Chilton Times* in 1868. Residents have taken notice of the German-speaking people who are building the St. Charles congregation in what will be become the village of Charlesburg. The news article allows us to see the developing community from the point of view of local residents.

The Chilton Times, July 25, 1868, on the Front Page

> The St. Charles Catholic Congregation – It is not generally known to our readers that there is a community, numbering 72 families of intelligent, enterprising and industrious Germans, 4 or 5 miles south of this village, in Eastern Brothertown, who have large clearings, good houses and barns, and are prospering as well as any community in the state. They were organized into a congregation in 1866 by Rev. Father Schroudenback, of this village, and ten acres of land was deeded, for church purposes, by Jacob Burg, of Marytown. On this ten acres this community have built a handsome hewn log house for the priest and a hewn log school house, each two stories high. The school house is now used for public worship, but in a short time these enterprising people intend to erect a stone church, ledges of beautiful limestone being near at hand.
>
> They have purchased a bell, which, with the hangings, weighs 1500 pounds, a large and beautiful mass book handsomely bound, with gilt edges and containing a large

number of steel engravings, a mass chalice, a communion chalice, an ostensorium or remonstrance, with incense and boat, a beautiful heavy satin veil trimmed with silver embroidery, a splendid statue of the blessed Virgin, having the child Jesus in her arms, a statue of St. Joseph, both being over four feet high, a superb funeral cross of brass, 2 crosses for the alter of carved wood, alter vestments, etc.

For some time their religious exercises were conducted by Rev. Father Pacificus, of Marytown, but they are now under the pastoral charge of Father Schroudenback, of this place, although they expect to have a pastor of their own as soon as Bishop Melcher assumes charge of this diocese. Taken altogether they are the most enterprising religious congregation in the county and their zeal in the faith they profess should be imitated in every community and by every denomination.[3]

The front-page article likely had *The Chilton Times* readership asking further questions about their new German-speaking neighbors:

- Where did these industrious, deeply religious German families originate?
- Who are these 72 families? What are their names?
- Why did our new German-speaking neighbors settle in Calumet County?

---

[3] "The St. Charles Catholic Congregation," *The Chilton Times*, 25 July 1868, front page. [transcribed by Joan Naomi Steiner, PhD]

Local and family historians have been trying to answer these questions, especially as they pertain to their ancestral origins. Families continue to write their stories of past generations for the benefit of future generations. Families also have diligently recorded from memory birthdates, marriages, and deaths. Today we have volumes of family histories. Some families also attempted to acquire their ancestors' actual birth and/or marriage records by writing letters to U.S. embassies in Europe. This process was slow, however, and not always fruitful.

Two 20th-century events in Europe remarkably changed how researchers of German-speaking people could acquire actual records to document their stories. Soviet-controlled regions in Europe opened to the world in 1989 with the fall of the Iron Curtain. The Velvet Revolution in today's Czech Republic resulted in freedom for its people. No longer did researchers need to work through U.S. embassies to acquire records to verify family information. Researchers could travel to these regions and access primary sources, including birth, marriage, death and land records.

Another critical development of the 1980s and 1990s was the rise of the internet. Many records once available only at state and regional archives were becoming digitized and available online to all with internet access. Today, local and family researchers have the option of working at archives or from anywhere in the world with internet access. Another important technological development for English-speaking researchers is computer-assisted technologies for translating typed materials written in other languages.

This book builds on the work of those who did not have the internet, digitized records or computer-assisted technologies. Local and family histories, as well as, family stories can now be documented with actual records of births, marriages and deaths from ancestral homelands. This unprecedented access affords researchers the opportunity to correct information, if needed, and to augment information by tracing ancestors as far back as records exist.

Chapter 1, "Finding Bohemia by Way of England," tells my personal connection to the developing village of Charlesburg as detailed in the 1868 news article published in *The Chilton Times*. I explain my family's misunderstandings about our origins.

An earlier version of this chapter was published by the German Bohemian Heritage Society of New Ulm, Minnesota.[4]

Chapter 2 introduces geographic locations of five Czech Republic parishes from which hundreds of German Bohemians emigrated. Their settlement areas in Wisconsin are also introduced.

Chapter 3, "The Wave of Immigration," lays out the research procedure used to uncover origins of German Bohemian families who settled in the Town of Brothertown and surrounding areas. An earlier version of this chapter also was published by the German Bohemian Heritage Society.[5]

Chapter 4 summarizes research findings about the five western Bohemian parishes in the study. In all, 570 German Bohemians are identified. Also, 322 German-speaking emigrants were discovered from 48 parishes not in the study. These newly-discovered emigrants and their origins are the impetus for further research.

---

[4] Steiner, Joan Naomi, PhD, "Finding Bohemia by Way of England," *Heimatbrief*, March 2019, 5-7. (available @ germanbohemianwisconsin.com)

[5] Steiner, Joan Naomi, PhD, "High Tide of High Hopes and Unlimited Opportunity," *Heimatbrief*, June/September 2020, 8-11. (available at https://germanbohemianwisconsin.com/)

The Conclusion summarizes the results of the research study and discusses why emigrants made Calumet County their settlement destination.

Part II is a repository of resources. Chapter 6 is a list of annotated local family and area histories. Chapter 7 is a list of video documentaries for Habakladrau and Pistau Parishes, Kladruby Chapel, and United States Embassy American Center Exhibition in Prague. Chapter 8 is a list of translated books about the region and its villages.

Chapter 9 introduces a local historian and his work in the Tepl and Marienbad areas. Books written in Czech are listed with English annotations that include family surnames and villages for in-depth descriptions of ancestral parishes and villages of German Bohemian families in the Town of Brothertown.

Chapter 10 discusses German resources, including books written in German. Each book listed is annotated in English with family surnames and villages from the research study. German and Czech points of view can be compared and contrasted with resources available in both languages.

This book provides answers to the questions Calumet County residents in 1868 likely would have asked after reading *The Chilton Times* news article:

- Where did these industrious, deeply religious German families originate?
- Who are these 72 families? What are their names?
- Why did they settle in Calumet County?

Resources in several languages offer various perspectives on the German Bohemian homeland of the Tepl and Marienbad areas. These books were gifts of Czech and German people whom I met through my research. Now, I pass on these gifts to others who want to learn more about the Town of Brothertown German Bohemians and their villages of origin.

Descendants of Calumet County's German Bohemians can be proud of their heritage. The many trials their ancestors faced and overcame must have deepened their religious faith. Their willingness to work hard and follow their dreams is revealed in their accomplishments as evidenced in daily life. Calumet County residents took notice and admired these hard-working, deeply religious German Bohemians who made the front page of *The Chilton Times* in 1868.

Chapter 1

Finding Bohemia By Way of England

In January 2016, I attended a British Institute in Salt Lake City, Utah, where it has been held for more than 20 years. Salt Lake City is home to the Family History Library (FHL), which makes possible online research through the website Familysearch.org.

My interest in attending the British Institute was to deepen my understanding of my maternal Maltby roots in Yorkshire and Somerset, England. I had signed up for a week-long study of English records since 1840. I also had requested an appointment with an FHL German consultant. My plan was to begin research on my paternal Steiner family's origins in Germany, with my German research to follow. However, by the end of my week-long English seminar, I had become totally absorbed with my father's roots. Since then, my Steiner ancestral homeland has been my central area of research.

Background

I grew up with my paternal grandfather, parents and brother on a 210-acre farm in Calumet County, Wisconsin, which is between Lake Michigan and Lake Winnebago in northeastern Wisconsin. Whenever my brother and I asked about the origins of our Steiner family, my father always told us we came from Germany. However, German was not spoken in our household. Grandma Steiner, who was, in part, English like my mother, insisted from the beginning of her marriage to my grandfather that English would be their home language.

In the 1990s, I acquired a copy of *The Descendants of Adalbert Steiner and Anna Guentner 1815-1886* compiled by Marianne Steiner.[1] Adalbert Steiner was my father's great-grandfather and Anna Guentner, his great-grandmother. The book includes a certified copy of Adalbert Steiner's death certificate stating that Adalbert was born in Germany.[2]

My great-great-grandfather, Adalbert Steiner, was born in Bohemia, today's Czech Republic.

The *Steiner* book also included a family lineage sheet for Adalbert.[3] His birth date was October 20, 1815, and his birth location on the lineage chart was listed as "Böhmen, Germany." Family stories, a death certificate and a family lineage page seemed to confirm for me that Adalbert Steiner, my great-great-grandfather, was born in Germany. These secondary sources served as my basis for requesting to meet with the FHL German consultant while I was attending the week-long British Institute. I did not know at the time of this meeting that Böhmen was a region under Austrian rule at the time of Adalbert's birth and immigration to the United States.

Family History Library

When I arrived at the library at my appointed time, the FHL Czech Republic consultant introduced herself to me, much to my surprise. She told me that my Steiner family originated from the Czech Republic, not Germany.

Henry and Alice Steiner's wedding portrait, October 21, 1913. My paternal German grandfather and grandmother.

I am sure the shocked expression on my face told her all she needed to know. As we talked, she helped me understand the conflict between my family's generational beliefs and the truth about their origins. She reminded me that Germany had not become a country until 1871. Böhmen, or Bohemia, the area identified as the birthplace of Adalbert in 1815, is located in the modern Czech Republic.

I was stunned. It felt as though everything that I had believed regarding the Steiner family's origins and ethnicity was in question. Luckily, for me, it was!

From the Czech Republic consultant, I learned that the *Steiner* name is a name of the "border people." She showed me a map and pointed to the area along the German-Czech border that she, as a native of the Czech Republic, considered the Bohemian border area. Using Familysearch online records for the Czech Republic, she showed me how to access baptismal church records that are available by parish and village. She found a Steiner family in one of the online parish records. I was given a list of recommended American sources that I needed to research before going to the Czech Republic records because, clearly, I did not know my ancestral village.

As my week of studying English records in Salt Lake City ended, I traveled home with far more questions about my so-called German ancestry. When I got home, I realized how little I knew about my grandfather, even though I had lived with him on our farm until he passed away when I was in my late teens. My father told me very little, probably because in the mid-to-late 1920s, when he was 10 or 11 years old, his mother, my part-English

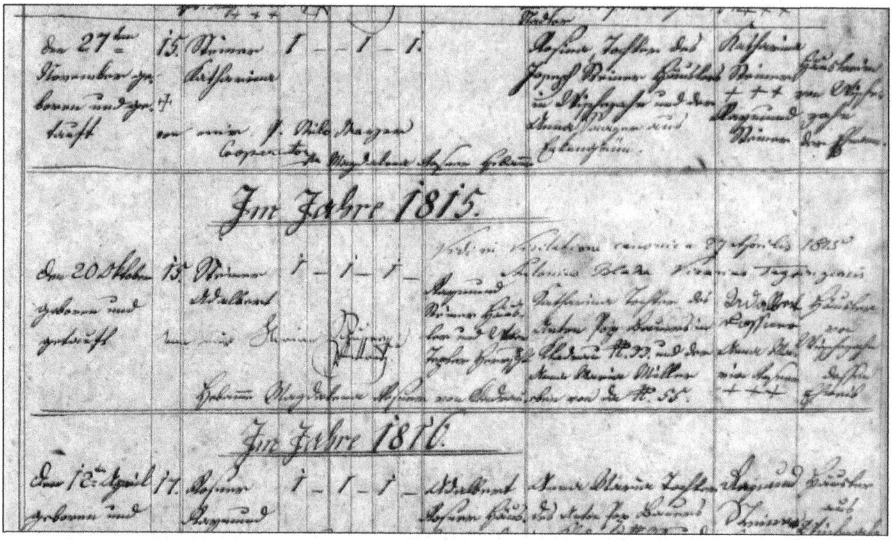
Im Jahre 1815.

Im Jahre 1816.

The baptismal record for my great-great-grandfather, Adalbert Steiner

---

grandmother, left the farm, her husband, and her son. I am sure this was a difficult time for him. I respected that he spoke little about it. What I learned about my father's situation came from my mother. She told me the Steiner family was Roman Catholic and that my grandfather had married an Episcopalian. According to my mother, after my grandparents' marriage, my grandfather had limited communication with the Steiner family. My father, as a result, grew up knowing the names of his grandparents, aunts and uncles, but not really knowing who they were. My brother and I knew even less.

The Work Begins

If I were ever going to locate my Steiner ancestral village, I realized that I would need to introduce myself to cousins I had never met. One cousin gave me the name of another cousin whom she thought had hired a genealogist years ago to locate the ancestral village. I emailed her, introduced myself and asked my questions. Much to my surprise, she gave me the village name of Wischezahn (known today as Vysočany) in the Parish of Habakladau (known today as Ovesné Kladruby), in the western part of the Czech Republic--along the border that the Czech consultant in Salt Lake City had pointed out to me. With that information, I went into the Familysearch Wiki to the Czech Republic and clicked on "Online Records" and found the Portafontium archives, just as the consultant had. I located the Habakladau Parish and the records for Wischezahn, my ancestral village. Because I knew Adalbert's birth date from his death certificate, I used the year, month and day to locate him in the records.

The previous image is the baptismal record for my great-great-grandfather Adalbert Steiner. Even though I had found the record, I was not able to read completely the German script of 1815.[4] I needed the entry translated, so that I could more completely understand the information.

In searching the internet, I found a genealogist in Prague who had experience in researching my homeland area of Habakladau. I contacted her business, and she agreed to translate Adalbert's baptismal record.

It reads:

Name:	**Steiner Adalbert**	
Religion:	Catholic	
Sex:	Male	
Status:	Legitimate	
Parents:		
Father:	**Raymund Steiner,** cottager and weaver, Tepl/Teplá dominion	
Mother:	**Katharina**, daughter of Anton **Pop**, peasant in Habakladrau/Ovesné Kladruby No. 33 and Anna Maria Miller just from there No. 55	
Godparents:		
Names:	Adalbert Rossner,	Anna Maria Rosner + + +
Social status:	Cottager from Wischezahn/Vysočany	his wife

Notes in the record: [Baptized] by me Marian Schusser [by my own hand], parish priest
Midwife Magdalena Rosner from Habakladrau/Ovesné Kladruby[5]

The translation offers valuable information:

- The names of my 3-times great-grandparents, Raymund and Katharina Steiner.
- The names of Katharina's parents (my 4-times great-grandparents) and her House No. 33 in Habakladau.

- The name of my 4-times great-grandmother Anna Maria Miller from House No. 55 in Habakladau.
- A note about Marian Schusser as the person who baptized Adalbert.
- The profession of Raymund Steiner, a cottager and weaver for the Tepl (known today as Teplá) dominion.

Learning the profession of my 3-times great-grandfather Raymund came as a surprise. I was not expecting to find this information in a baptismal record. Not knowing what a "cottager and weaver" meant, I consulted a book entitled *Heimatbrief: Stories of German-Bohemians.*

One of the stories, "Peasants in Bohemia," offered me insights into the life of my 3-times great-grandfather Raymund Steiner as a cottager and a weaver:

> A cottager had no land at all. The more fortunate cottager had a shed or lean-to with a goat and a few chickens but most of them were at the bottom of the economic ladder—day laborers and weavers or cloth finishers and dyers....A true cottage was a freestanding small residence, often only one room but possibly with a loft of some kind.[6]

I learned that Raymund and Katharina Steiner likely did not own land. Tax records and land records may confirm what they owned if anything. House No. 15 in Wischezahn was probably small, with a weaver's loom, thread and/or yarn, and other related work tools. Such was the household that Adalbert was born into on October 20, 1815.

As I studied the translation, questions arose from the bits and pieces of information found in the record:

- Who are the Rossner/Rosner godparents? Were they relatives? What do the three crosses after Anna Marie's name represent?
- What was the relationship between Magdalena Rosner and the Rossner/Rosner godparents?
- What was the role of the midwife in small Bohemian villages like Wischezahn, especially in relationship to the priest?
- What was the "dominion" mentioned in the record? How was " dominion" related to Habakladau and Wischezahn?
- Had the family church survived?

These questions were clearly about my desire to build a context in which my Steiner family lived, worked and died. I wanted to know them through their work, their daily lives, their disappointments and their celebrations. I needed to become acquainted with their social, economic, and political reality of the 1800s.

Next Steps

I located Adalbert's baptism record while working at home on August 8, 2016. Anyone who has broken through a brick wall knows the feelings: stunned, excited, relieved, and exuberant all at once! I will never forget that day. This discovery was the impetus for my next steps. I wanted to locate House No. 15 in Wischezahn in the Parish of Habakladau on a map and begin to learn about the history of the area. I was beginning to see that my ancestors' story *is* my story! Thanks to the British Institute in Salt Lake City and my meeting with the Czech Republic consultant at the Family History Library, I found Bohemia by way of England!

Reference Notes:

[1] Steiner, Marianne, compiler. *The Descendants of Adalbert Steiner and Anna Guentner [Gintner] 1815-1886 (*Humboldt, SK: Privately printed, 1986).

[2] Steiner, *Descendants* 19.

[3] Steiner, *Descendants* 25.

[4] Portafontium. Ovesné Kladruby," no. 5, Adalbert Steiner entry, October 20, 1815, accessed August 8, 2016, https://www.portafontium.eu/iipimage/30066841/ovesne-kladruby-05_0810-n?x=356&y=167&w=866&h=520.

[5] Jan and Renata Peez, May 8, 2018, www.pathfinders.cz.

[6] Hobbs, Karen, "Peasants in Bohemia," in German-Bohemian Heritage Society, editor, *Heimatbrief: Stories of German-Bohemians, (*New Ulm, MN: Edinborough Press, 2013), p. 147.

Chapter 2

Where Did the German-Speaking Emigrants Originate?

Western Bohemia

Beginning in the 1850s, more than 570 German Bohemian emigrants made Calumet County, Wisconsin, their destination. At the time, western Bohemia was part of the Kingdom of Bohemia. German-speaking emigrants from western Bohemia are known today as German Bohemians. The German Bohemians lived along the borders of today's Czech Republic and are sometimes referred to as the Border People.

Map 1: Czech Republic[2]

Today's Czech Republic

Today's Czech Republic was constituted in 1993.[1] Map 1 shows the countries bordering the Czech Republic: Poland on the north, Slovakia on the east, Austria on the south, and Germany on the west and northwest. German Bohemian families lived on the borderlands until German-speaking people were expelled after World War II.

---

[1] Encyclopedia Britannica (https://www,briticannica.com/place/Czech-Republic/History: accessed 20 May 2022), "Czech Republic History."

[2] Maps Czech Republic- Czechoslovakia. Digital image (https://maps-czech-republic.com/maps-czech-republic---czechoslovakia-in-world/czech-republic-map-and-surrounding-countries: accessed 20 May 2022)

German-Speaking Areas

German-speaking people populated the border areas of the Czech Republic until the end of World War II. Map 2 shows areas with the highest concentration of German-speaking people in 1910 court districts. The darker blue areas point to the most heavily populated areas of native German speakers. The Expulsion after World War II emptied the borderland of German speakers. Chapter 10 will discuss the Expulsion and its effects on today's Czech borderlands.

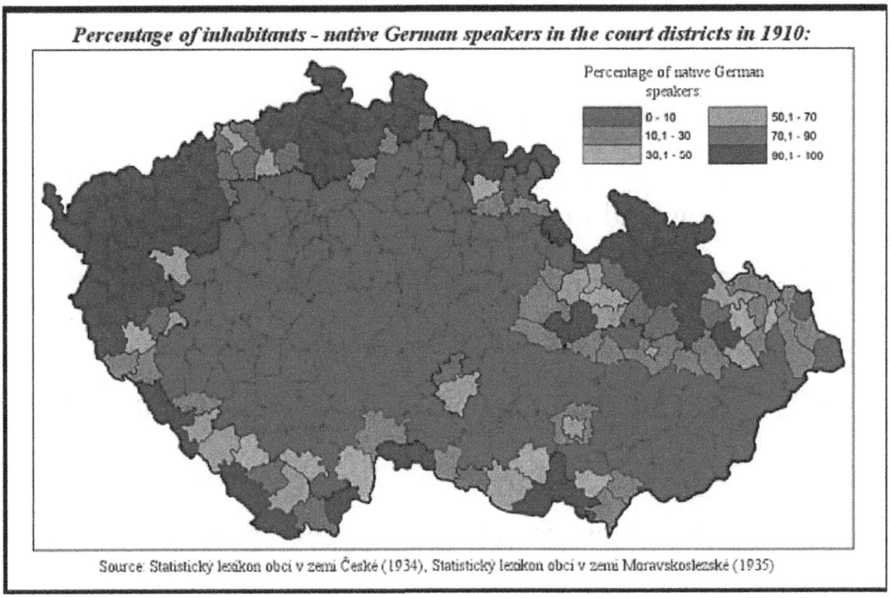

Map 2: Percentage of inhabitants[3]

[3] Statistický lexicon obec v zemi České (1934), Statistický lexicon obec v zemi Moravskodlezské (1935).

Map 3: German Bohemian Homeland[4]

Tepl and Marienbad Areas

Tepl and Marienbad area villages are located along the border of northwestern Bohemia. These villages were part of the Tepl Monastery Estate during feudal times. The Tepl Monastery Estate had oversight of approximately 50 villages.[5] The feudal system required serfs to work lands of the estate. Serfs lived under the rules of the estate. Map 3 with German placenames shows the Tepl and Marienbad areas with many surrounding area vil-

---

[4] *Map of Kaiserwald und Tepler Hochland Die Kreife: Marienbad-Plan-Tepl.* Nürmberg: Helmut Preußler Veriag + Druck. 1989. Privately held by Joan Naomi Steiner, PhD [ADDRESS FOR PRIVATE USE,] Neenah, Wisconsin, June 2019.

[5] František Palacký, Popis Králowstwí českého, čili, Podrobné poznamenání wšech. (1848), 402-403.

lages which would have made up, in part, the Tepl Monastery Estate. The map pinpoints ancestral villages of German Bohemians settling in Calumet County beginning in the 1850s. Hundreds of emigrants left this region, creating a large wave of immigration to Calumet County, Wisconsin.

Calumet County, Wisconsin

German Bohemians immigrated to Calumet County, especially the Town of Brothertown, to establish a new life for themselves, their family and future generations. Map 4 is a Wisconsin map from 1846, two years before statehood. The forested area offered fertile farmland with a climate similar to that of western Bohemia. Surrounding waterways of the Great Lakes, Lake Winnebago and the Fox and Manitowoc rivers made for excellent transportation, which would be important for selling grains and other farm products.

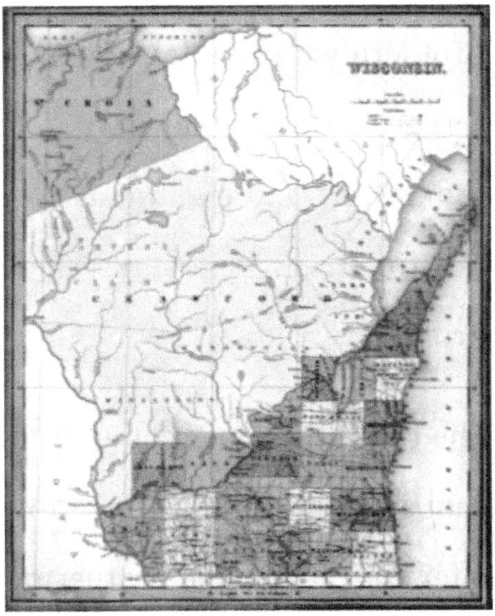

Map 4: Wisconsin 1846[6]

[6] *S. Augustus Mitchell, Wisconsin 1846 (Philadelphia: S. Augustus Mitchell, 1846). Digital image, American Geographical Society Library, University of Wisconsin-Milwaukee Libraries (https://collections.lib.uwm.edu/digital/collection/agdm/id/654/rec/2: accessed 20 May 2022).*

Town of Brothertown

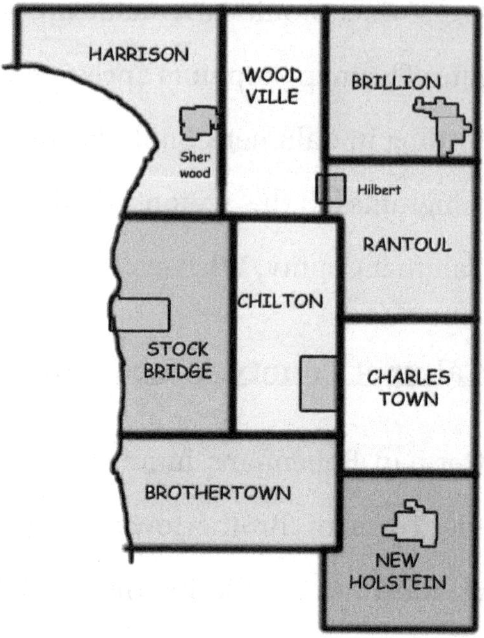

Map 5: Towns of Calumet County[9]

Towns in Wisconsin as government structures were established in 1827, when Wisconsin was a territory.[7] The United States government in 1839 granted land known as the Town of Brothertown (save for 500 acres) to the Brothertown Indians, who were emigrating from New York state. The Town of Brothertown became the Brothertown Reservation.[8]

The U.S. government offered citizenship to tribal members in exchange for their willingness to own an allotment of acreage. The offer appealed to the Brothertown Indians, who had moved several times from previous homelands. Unfortunately, some tribal members lost their land for nonpayment of taxes. Land specula-

---

[7] *"Structures of Government," Encyclopedia of Government (ECM) a digital library held at the UWM. (https://emke.uwm.edu/entry/structure-of-local-government/: accessed 20 May 2022).*

[8] *Cipolla, Craig, and Caroline Andler. "The Brothertown Indian Nation History." History: A Brief Historical Overview Fond du Lac, Wisconsin: Brothertown Indian Nation; (https://brothertownindians.org/heritage/history/: accessed 20 May 2022).*

[9] *Historical Atlas of Wisconsin (Milwaukee: Snyder, Van Vechten and Co., 1846), Digital image (http://sites.rootsweb.com/~wicalume/: accessed 10 May 2022).*

tors bought up the land and resold it.[10] Map 5 shows the towns of Calumet County.

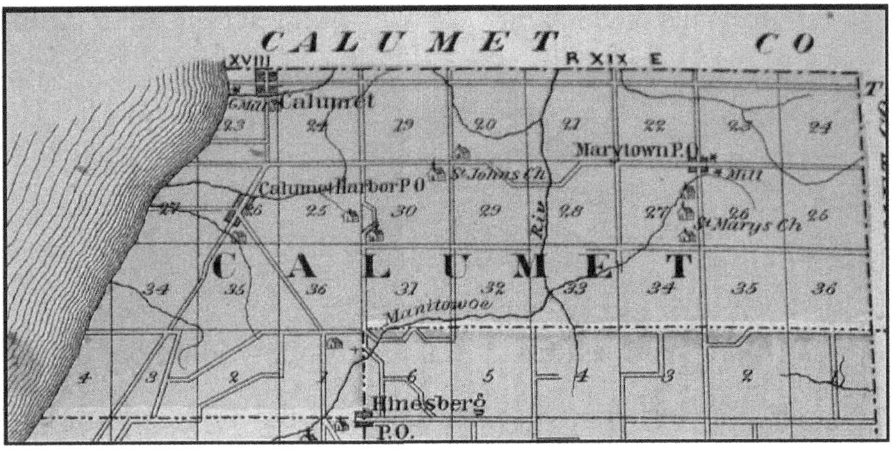

Map 6: Town of Calumet, Fond du Lac County 1846[11]

Marytown, Town of Calumet in Fond du Lac County

Several early German Bohemian settlers, my Steiner family included, first stayed at Marytown in the Town of Calumet in Fond du Lac County before buying land in the Town of Brothertown. Marytown, which was organized as a parish in 1849, was known to Roman Catholics through Bishop Henni from Milwaukee. Bishop Henni recruited German immigrants to Wisconsin.

---

[10] *Cipolla, Craig, and Caroline Andler. "The Brothertown Indian Nation History." History: A Brief Historical Overview Fond du Lac, Wisconsin: Brothertown Indian Nation; (https://brothertownindians.org/heritage/history/ : accessed 20 May 2022.)*

[11] *Illustrated Historical Map of Wisconsin (Milwaukee: Snyder, Van Vechten & Co. 1878), Digital image (http://www.formycousins.com/1878/1878atlas-Fondulac.html : accessed 20 May 2022).*

Early German Bohemians who settled in the Town of Brothertown walked about 5 miles to St. Mary's Church in Marytown for weekly church services until they could build their own church.[12] Map 6 (previous page) shows Marytown in relationship to Calumet County.

Conclusion

German Bohemian settlers of Calumet County identified in the research study originated from villages in the Tepl and Marienbad areas along the western border of today's Czech Republic. Most settled in the Town of Brothertown in Calumet County. These industrious German-speaking immigrants came directly to Wisconsin to buy land, clear timber for fields, build homes and establish their church and school. The German Bohemians from the Tepl and Marienbad areas came to Calumet County to build a better life for themselves and their families for generations to come.

---

[12] *John Kern, A History of the Parish of St. Charles Borromeo from its Beginning to 1866 to the Days of Diamond Jubilee November 4, 1941, (Privately printed, 1941).*

Chapter 3

High Tide of High Hopes and Unlimited Opportunities: The Research Study

Background

The year 1848 was a landmark year for both the Marienbad and Tepl area villages in northwestern Bohemia and in Wisconsin. People from the Marienbad and Tepl area villages were released from the centuries-old feudal system when it collapsed in 1848. That new-found freedom likely filled the hearts and minds of people with hope for a better future for themselves and their families.

The year 1848 brought Wisconsin statehood and new hope for a promising future, as well. New settlers would be needed to help turn the wilderness into a proud and productive state. Wisconsin's bountiful forests and rich farmland offered emigrants from the Marienbad and Tepl area villages opportunities to begin new lives filled with prospects for a better future.

Both German Bohemian immigrants who settled in Wisconsin and their relatives who remained in the homeland began to embrace democracy. Through democratic processes, they developed a strong civil society in the new world and in the homeland. The year 1848 marks a high tide of high hopes and unlimited opportunities on both sides of the Atlantic Ocean.

In this promising context, Calumet County and the Town of Brothertown, Wisconsin, was soon to be settled by German Bohemians emigrating from the Marienbad and Tepl area villages.

How It All Began

I began to see patterns of familiar surnames on christening, marriage and death records in parish books as I researched my Steiner family ancestors. Soon I was making family surname connections

Looking north from left to right on this postcard are St. Charles Rectory, Church and School in Calumet County, Wisconsin, in 1908. (Herb Buhl collection)[1]

between villages in northwestern Bohemia and my hometown area of Charlesburg, Town of Brothertown, Calumet County. I learned from the St. Charles Church history, *A History of the Parish of St. Charles Borromeo*, the names of the first settlers of the area. They were German Bohemians from the Marienbad and Tepl area villages who arrived in the Town of Brothertown before my Steiner ancestors in 1856. I didn't know that at the time.

As more families arrived, they bought land, built their first homes and established their new village. They called their new village *Charlesburg*. The German Bohemians built a church, rectory and school under the name of St. Charles. In 1858, according to the church history, German Bohemian settlers established St. Charles Cemetery on the north side of their church.[2]

The St. Charles Church history also identified by name the first settlers of Charlesburg. I located their villages of origin and birth and/or christening records through online research.

Each German Bohemian first settler is listed below:

- Anton Reinl was born in Abaschin, No. 3, Egerland, Bohemia, Austria-Hungary (now Závišín, okres Cheb, Karlovarský kraj, Česko).[3]
- Raymond Lodes was born in Rojau, No. 19, Egerland, Bohemia, Austria-Hungary (now Rájov, okres Cheb, Karlovarský kraj, Česko).[4]
- Joseph Nadler was born in Rojau, No. 66, Egerland, Bohemia, Austria-Hungary (now Rájov, okres Cheb, Karlovarský kraj, Česko).[5]
- Joseph Fischer was born in Rojau, No. 8, Egerland, Bohemia, Austria-Hungary (now Rájov, okres Cheb, Karlovarský kraj, Česko).[6]

All four families traveled from the port of Bremen, Germany, to the port of New York. The Lodes family arrived in 1854;[7] the other three families arrived in 1855.[8] Their letters home likely encouraged other families from the Marienbad and Tepl area villages, like my Steiner family, to join them. Over the next several decades, hundreds of German Bohemians arrived in Calumet County, resulting in a wave of German Bohemian immigration from the Marienbad and Tepl area villages.

Looking east toward Prague, which is about 94 miles away, this aerial view of the Tepl Monastery appeared on a historic postcard. (Joan Naomi Steiner, PhD, collection)

The Beginnings of an Immigration Research Project

My family research grew into the Calumet County Immigration Research Project. The geographic scope of this project included villages in the following Tepl Monastery parishes in the Marienbad and Tepl areas (both German and Czech placenames are given): Habakladrau (now Ovesné Kladruby); Pistau (now Pistov);

Einsiedl (now Mnichov); Tepl (now Teplá); and Rojau (now Rájov). The research method and procedure used to uncover German Bohemian immigrants follows:

- German Bohemian immigrants were identified from a list of people buried in St. Charles Cemetery.
- Information about the identified German Bohemian immigrants was gathered from county and state records, local newspaper obituaries and family histories in local libraries.
- Online immigration records were located for identified German Bohemian immigrants.
- Naturalization records were used to trace identified German Bohemian immigrants to their parish or village when possible.
- Online birth records of identified German Bohemian immigrants were located using the online State Regional Archive in Pilsen (now Plzen).
- Links to original records with each identified German Bohemian immigrant were entered into an online data base at germanbohemianwisconsin.com.
- Reports of identified German Bohemian immigrants by their birth or christening village were generated. Chapter 4 includes the reports and discusses the findings.

At the time of this writing, more than 400 German Bohemians from Marienbad and Tepl area villages relocated to Calumet County, Wisconsin. Surnames include, but are not limited to: Denk, Fischbach, Fischer, Gintner, Groeschl, Hammer, Leitner, Lenz, Lodes, Muller, Nadler, Neubauer, Pimpl, Pop, Popp, Reinl, Rott, Rummer, Schott, Schusser, Steiner, Utschig, Weber, Wettstein and Zucker.

Further Research

Each year the Sudeten Germans, many of them living relatives of the Wisconsin German Bohemians, from the Marienbad and Tepl area villages, have a reunion at Der Heiligenhof in Bad Kissingen, Germany. I attended the reunion in June 2019. I shared drafts of my research, which included surnames and villages of German Bohemians who emigrated from their home areas beginning in 1850. Several people shared recollections of hearing family stories about relatives who immigrated to the United States. One woman remembered letters that were sent back and forth. She remembered that they settled in Jericho, Wisconsin, which also is located in the Town of Brothertown in Calumet County. The Sudeten Germans at the reunion were interested in finding out more about their relatives who settled in Calumet County.

I also attended the Kirchenfest St. Laurentius in Habakladrau and the Reunion of Bartholomäus-Fest in Pistau in the Czech Republic in August 2019. Video documentaries of these events are listed in Part II of this book. Some of the Sudeten Germans from the Bad Kissingen Reunion also attended.

We continued our dialogue about the German Bohemians who settled in Calumet County. The Sudeten Germans shared books and copies of research materials about Habakladrau and Pistau area villages. Their gifts of information have added invaluable depth to my research. These resources are included in Part II of this book. We remain in contact, using email and Google Translate.

During my August 2019 visit to the Czech Republic, I met with mayors, local historians and community members to share preliminary findings of my research showing the wave of immigration to Wisconsin. Local leaders took great interest in learning more about former residents of their villages who had emigrated from the area. They were pleased to think that other Wisconsin German Bohemian descendants might be interested in visiting their villages in the future.

Next Steps

These are the next steps needed to continue the research:

1. Immigration findings need to be compiled and distributed to descendants of Calumet County German Bohemian immigrants, Sudeten Germans and their descendants from Marienbad and Tepl areas and Czech residents living in Marienbad and Tepl area villages.
2. A greater awareness of common cultural ties needs to be built among descendants of Wisconsin German Bohemians, Sudeten Germans and their descendants, and Czechs living in area villages.
3. Other interested Calumet County German Bohemian descendants, like myself, need to be located so that they, too, can share their ancestors' untold stories.

As this work continues, I welcome all Calumet County German Bohemian descendants to help uncover more about the German Bohemian settlement in Calumet County, Wisconsin. Their story is only beginning to be told.

Direct beneficiaries of this work include Sudetenland Germans and their descendants; Czech residents and their descendants; and Calumet County, Wisconsin, descendants. The direct benefit to all is learning about and appreciating our common German Bohemian roots and heritage. We all benefit from knowing the untold story of our ancestors.

Reference Notes:

1 Kern, John. *A History of the Parish of St. Charles Borromeo from its beginning in 1866 to the days of its Diamond Jubilee November 4, 1941*. Privately held by Joan Naomi Steiner, PhD [ADDRESS FOR PRIVATE USE,] Neenah, Wisconsin, 2005.

2 Postcard of St. Charles Church, Rectory, and School, 1908. From the Postcard Collection. Privately held by Herb Buhl, [ADDRESS FOR PRIVATE USE,] Chilton, Wisconsin, January 2016.

3 Roman Catholic Church (Habakladrau, Egerland, Bohemia, Austria-Hungary (currently, Ovesné Kladruby, Cheb, Czech Republic). Parish registers, 1814-1866. Book 5, image 134, page 270, line 1, Digital Images. State Regional Archive in Pilsen (Plzen). https://www.portafontium.eu/iipimage/30066841/ovesne-kladruby-05_1350-n?x=24&y=36&w=482&h=203 : 2019.

4 Roman Catholic Church (Rojau, Egerland, Bohemia, Austria-Hungary (currently, Rájov, Cheb, Karlovarsky, Czech Republic). Parish Registers, 1789-1840. Book 1, image 46, page 87, Line 4. Digital Images. State Regional Archive in Pilsen (Plzen). https://www.portafontium.eu/iipimage/30067855/rajov-01_0461-n?x-=419&y=340&w=615&h=259 : 2019.

5 Roman Catholic Church (Rojau, Egerland, Bohemia, Austria-Hungary (currently, Rájov, Cheb, Karlovarsky, Czech Republic). Parish Registers, 1789-1840, Book 1, image 55, page 90, Line1. Digital Images. State Regional Archive in Pilsen (Plzen). https://www.portafontium.eu/iipimage/30067855/rajov-01_0551-n?x=-22&y=65&w=753&h=317 : 2019.

6 Roman Catholic Church (Rojau, Egerland, Bohemia, Austria-Hungary (currently, Rájov, Cheb, Karlovarsky, Czech Republic). Parish Registers, 1789-1840. Book 1, Page 116, Image 75. Line 3. Digital Images. State Regional Archive in Pilsen (Plzen). https://www.portafontium.eu/iipimage/30067855/rajov-01_0751-n?x=-22&y=269&w=586&h=246 . 2019.

7 *Passenger Lists of Vessels Arriving at New York, New York, 1820-1897.* Microfilm Publication M237, 675 rolls. NAI: 6256867. Records of the U.S. Customs Service, Record Group 36. National Archives at Washington, D.C. Database. *Ancestry.com*, (http://www.ancestry.com : accessed 21 November 2019), entry for R. Ludes [Lodes], age 46, arrived New York Castle Gardens, 14 September 1854 aboard the *Elizabeth*.

8 *Passenger Lists of Vessels Arriving at New York, New York, 1820-1897.* Microfilm Publication M237, 675 rolls. NAI: 6256867. Records of the U.S. Customs Service, Record Group 36. National Archives at Washington, D.C. Database. *Ancestry.com*, (http://www.ancestry.com : accessed 21 November 2019), entries for Franz T. [J.] Nadler, age 39; Anton Reindel [Reinl] age 30; Joseph Fischer, age 30 arrived New York Castle Gardens, 31 November 1855 aboard the *Meta*.

Chapter 4

Summary of Research Findings

The Calumet County Immigration Research Study identified emigrants from the Marienbad and Tepl area parishes. A total of 570 emigrants were identified. Of those, 248 emigrated from the five targeted parishes of the Tepl and Marienbad areas: Habakladrau (now Ovesné Kladruby); Pistau (now Pistov); Einsiedl (now Mnichov), Tepl (now Teplá); and Rojau (now Rájov).

Limitations of the Study

The study used parish and village birth and christening records when available to determine an immigrant's origin. However, those records can be imprecise. Expectant mothers, for example, typically returned to their mother's home to give birth. The newborn's birth and/or christening record then was located in the grandmother's parish.

In other cases, some parish record books were not online. The books may not have survived, or if they did, the records may not have been digitized. Record release laws in the Czech Republic also may have made it impossible to obtain records. These circumstances necessitated the use of U.S. records as evidence for places of origin supported with other family member's evidence. However, for the most part, the researcher was able to obtain actual birth and/or christening records for emigrants.

Immigrants who first arrived in Wisconsin are included in the study even though they may have continued westward to buy land in other states, including Iowa, Minnesota and the Dakotas. Immigrants whose original destination was Wisconsin were counted for the purposes of this study.

Several immigrants are listed twice in the study because their spouses died, and they remarried. Even though they are listed twice, they are counted only once. A single asterisk indicates they married twice. For emigrants who traveled more than once to the United States, a double asterisk is used. They are listed twice but counted only once.

Database for Repository of Records

Records documenting immigrants include, but are not limited to, the following U.S records: Immigration and Naturalization; 1860, 1870, and 1880 U.S. Census; property and tax; obituaries; and local family histories. Record citations and links to actual records for individual immigrants are held in a database at https://www.germanbohemianwisconsin.com/.

The actual birth and/or christening and marriage records for individuals in the database, for example, are obtained by clicking on the link http://www.portafontium.eu/contents/register/soap-pn/cirkev-rimskokatolicka in the individual's profile. Likewise, burial information in the profile is obtained by clicking on the link https://www.findagrave.com/. All sources are fully cited in the database.

Emigrants by Parish

In all, 248 identified emigrants were born and/or christened in the five targeted parishes. The following table shows the number of emigrants by parish (place names are listed in German and Czech) and the percentage (rounded up) each parish contributed to the total number of emigrants:

Distribution of Emigrants by Parish in Study

Parish Name	Number of Emigrants	% of Emigrants by Targeted Parish
Royau/Rájov	77	31%
Habakladrau/Ovesné Kladruby	70	28%
Einsiedl/Mnichov	57	23%
Tepl Stadt/Teplá Mesto	30	12%
Pistau/Pistov	14	6%
Total	**248**	**100%**

In summary, 248 people emigrated from the study's five parishes. Emigrants from these five parishes make up 44% of all emigrants identified.

The following table shows villages by parish from which emigrants originated. The percentage of emigrants by parish village shows the percentage each village contributed to the total number from each parish.

Distribution of Emigrants by Parish and Village in Study

Parish	Parish Emi-grants	Parish Village	Village Emigrants	% of Emigrants by Parish Village
Royau/Rájov	77			
		Royau/Rájov	77	100%
Habakladrau/ Ovesné Kladruby	70			
		Abaschin/ Závišín	8	11%
		Habakladrau/ Ovesné Kladruby	37	53%
		Hohendorf/ Zádub	1	1%
		Müllestau/ Milhostov	5	7%
		Wischezahn/ Vysočany	12	17%
		Wischkowitz/ Výškovice	7	10%
Einsiedl/Mnichov	57			
		Einsiedl/ Mnichov	33	58%
		Kschiha/Čihaná	15	26%
		Pfaffengrün/ Popovice	1	2%
		Rauschenbach/ Sítiny	8	14%
Tepl Stadt/Teplá Mesto	30			
		Böhmisch Borau/Beranov	1	3%
		Enkengrün/ Jankovice	9	30%
		Lusading/ Sluzetin	7	23%

Parish	Parish Emi-grants	Parish Village	Village Emigrants	% of Emigrants by Parish Village
		Pauten/Poutnov	4	13%
		Pobitz/Babice	2	7%
		Tepl Stadt/ Teplá Mesto	7	23%
Pistau/Pistov	14			
		Martinau/ Martinov	8	57%
		Wilkowitz/ Vlkovice	6	43%
Total	**248**		**248**	

The research process uncovered 322 emigrants from parishes in the Marienbad and Tepl areas other than the five parishes in the study. The following table lists 48 parishes and the number of emigrants from each parish not in the study.

Distribution of Emigrants by Parish Not in Study

Parish Name	Number of Emigrants
Albersdörfer Brand/Milíře	6
Auherzen/Úherce	11
Auschowitz/Úšovice	4
Bleistadt/Oloví	3
Chlum Svate Mari/Chlum Svaté Maří	27
Chodau/Chodov	7
Donawitz/Stanovice	2
Elbogen/Locket	2

Parish Name	Number of Emigrants
Falkenau/Sokolov	1
Frohnau/Vranov	7
Girsh/Krsy	7
Gossengrün/Krajková	1
Graslitz/Kraslice	13
Habersbirk/Habartov	1
Heiligenkreuz/Chodský Újezd	6
Hohen-Zetish/Vysoké Sedliště	18
Kapsch/Skapce	2
Kirchenbirk/Kosteini Briza	5
Königsberg/Kynšperk nad Ohří	2
Kosolup/Kozolupy	8
Kostelzen/Kostelec	7
Kumerau/Komárov	2
Landek/Otročín	2
Lanz/Lomnice	5
Leskau/Lestkov	18
Lobs/Lobzy	6
Marienbad/Mariánské Lázně	9
Neudek/Nejdek	1
Neudorf/Nová Ves	13
Neudorf/Trstěnice	4
Ober Kozolup/Horní Kozolupy	8
Ober-Sekeřan v/vHorní Sekyřany	2
Ottenreuth/Otín	15
Pfraumberg/Přimda	6
Pilsen/Plzeň	1
Prostibor/Prostiboř	4
Punnau/Boněnov	4
Sankt Adalbert/Svatý Vojěch	19
Schönwald/Lesná	6
Tachau/Tachov	6
Tepl Stift/Teplá Klaster	3
Theusing/Toužim	8
Trinkseifen/Rudné	7

Parish Name	Number of Emigrants
Tschernoschin/Černošín	2
Tutz/Dubec	18
Unter Jammy/Dolní Jamné	1
Welperschitz/Erpužice	9
Witschin/Vidžín	3
Total	**322**

In summary, 322 emigrants, or 56%, were identified from parishes not in the scope of the research study.

Summary of Findings

The wave of immigration to Calumet County, Wisconsin, from the Tepl and Marienbad areas in western Bohemia began in the early 1850s. German Bohemians settled in and around today's Charlesburg in the Town of Brothertown and expanded to other areas in Calumet County. Research discovered the following:

- 44% of emigrants identified originate from five targeted parishes in the study.
- 56% of emigrants identified originate from parishes in the Marienbad and Tepl areas that were not targeted for the study.

Need for Further Study

- Continue to research and obtain actual birth and/or christening records as they become available online and/or in state and national archives in the Czech Republic.
- Expand the Calumet County Immigration Research Study to include the 48 parishes in the Marienbad and Tepl areas not in the original study.
- Expand parish and village histories found in Part II of this book for emigrants who originated from parishes and villages not targeted for the original study.

Summary

Many German Bohemian descendants from Calumet County, Wisconsin, like my family, believe that their ancestors came from Germany because that is what our families believed. Our ancestors were German-speaking people. Germany, however, did not become a nation until 1871. Not until online records became accessible to researchers were we able to locate birth and/or christening records to identify correctly ancestral origins. The immigration findings need to be distributed to Calumet County German Bohemian descendants who have ancestral roots in the Tepl and Marienbad areas. Some family histories and local histories may need to be expanded or rewritten, given these findings.

Places and abbreviations

United States burial states and counties for selected states:

California = CA

Iowa-Delaware = IA-D
Iowa-Harrison = IA-HR
Iowa-Palo Alto = IA-PA
Iowa-Shelby = IA-S
Iowa-Story = IA-St

Illinois = IL

Indiana = IN

Kansas = KS

Massachusetts = MA

Missouri = MO

Minnesota-Benton = MN-Be
Minnesota-Brown = MN-B
Minnesota-Cottonwood = MN-C
Minnesota-Hubbard = MN-H
Minnesota-Nicollet = MN-N
Minnesota-Ramsey = MN-RA
Minnesota-Redwood = MN-RW
Minnesota-Renville = MN-RN
Minnesota-Rice = MN-R
Minnesota-Stearns = MN-S
Minnesota-Traverse = MN-TR
Minnesota-Wilkin = MN-WL

Nebraska = NE

North Dakota = ND

New Jersey = NJ

New York = NY

Ohio = OH

Oregon = OR

Pennsylvania = PA

South Dakota = SD

Washington = WA

Wisconsin-Barron = WI-B
Wisconsin-Brown = WI-BR
Wisconsin-Calumet = WI-C
Wisconsin-Clark = WI-Cl
Wisconsin-Dodge = WI-D
Wisconsin-Door = WI-DR
Wisconsin-Fond du Lac = WI-FDL
Wisconsin-Jackson = WI-J
Wisconsin-Manitowoc = WI-Mw
Wisconsin-Marathon = WI-Mar
Wisconsin-Milwaukee = WI-M
Wisconsin-Outagamie = WI-O
Wisconsin-Ozaukee = WI-OZ
Wisconsin-Racine = WI-R
Wisconsin-Shawano = WI-SH
Wisconsin-Sheboygan = WI-S
Wisconsin-Washington = WI-WA
Wisconsin-Winnebago = WIN
Wisconsin-Wood = WI-W

Canada = CAN

Record Types:
B = Baptismal and/or Christening Record
MARR = Marriage Record
TBV = To Be Verified

Special Designations:
Bef = Before
Abt = About
Aft = After
*Name = Multiple marriages
**Name = Multiple trips to United States

The Wave of Emigration Beginning in 1850 from Tepla Land, Bohemia and Surrounding Areas to Calumet County, Wisconsin - Research Study

Arrival in U.S.A.	Name	Born/Baptised	House No.	Spouse	Died	Burial	Record Types
PARISH - Einsiedl / Mnichov							
Einsiedl / Mnichov							
31 Jan 1837	Zitterbart, Fidelis	20 Apr 1804	002	Frederica Olnhausen	1887	PA	B
13 Sep 1852	Zitterbart, Louis	9 Jan 1838	030	Philomina Keller	6 Aug 1899	PA	B
29 Oct 1853	Utschig, Johann	29 Dec 1799	008	Maria Elisabeth Schicker			B
Nov 1853	Schurwon, Toletta	13 Jun 1812	107	Rochus Zitterbart	1895	PA	B
Nov 1853	Zitterbart, Anna	2 Jan 1848	018		1929		B
Nov 1853	Zitterbart, Catherine	19 Jul 1850	100				B
Nov 1853	Zitterbart, Rochus	18 Jul 1810	002	Toletta Schurwon	13 Jan 1894	PA	B
30 Jul 1855	Christel, Amalia	6 Apr 1819	016	Norbert Christoph Christl	1 Nov 1902	WI-Mw	B
30 Jul 1855	Christl, Adolph	4 Jan 1850	127		30 Jan 1882		B
30 Jul 1855	Christl, Augusta	3 Oct 1840	127	Peter Hartman	6 Apr 1915	WI-Mw	B
30 Jul 1855	Christl, Ernestine	21 Mar 1832	016	Joseph Loeb	Bef 1900		B
30 Jul 1855	Christl, Johann	10 Aug 1843	127		12 Jun 1886		B
30 Jul 1855	Christl, Karl B	8 May 1847	127		8 Dec 1924	WI-M	B
30 Jul 1855	Christl, Louis Melchoir	5 Jan 1855	127		27 Apr 1929	MN-Be	B
30 Jul 1855	Christl, Norbert Christoph	25 Jul 1811	127	Maria Anna Amalia Ziedler	1 Apr 1897	WI-Mw	B
30 Jul 1855	*Christl, Norbert Christoph	25 Jul 1811	127	Amalia Christel	1 Apr 1897	WI-Mw	B
30 Jul 1855	Christl, Richard F	7 Feb 1842	127		23 Mar 1925	WI-Mw	B
30 Jul 1855	Christl, Theodore Isador F	28 Feb 1845	127		23 Nov 1937	MN-Be	B
30 Jul 1855	Christl, Wendel	9 Dec 1851	127		2 Nov 1922	WI-Mw	B
30 Jul 1855	Groeschl, Anna	3 Aug 1851	109		3 Jul 1890	WI-C	B

30 Jul 1855	Groeschl, Franziska	9 Jun 1854	107				B
30 Jul 1855	Groeschl, Johann	20 Jun 1823	109	Thekla Zucker	12 Jun 1873	WI-C	B
30 Jul 1855	Treml, Ludmilla	27 Jan 1832	081		9 Jan 1923	IA-St	B
30 Jul 1855	Utschig, Albert	21 Oct 1830	030	Anna Klapperich	1 Apr 1911	WI-C	B
30 Jul 1855	Utschig, August	19 May 1828	030	Catharine Nett	5 Apr 1903	WI-FDL	B
30 Jul 1855	Zucker, Thekla	5 Aug 1826	048	Johann Groeschl	17 Jan 1899	WI-C	B
1 Sep 1855	Loeb, Joseph	1 Jan 1827		Ernestine Christl	12 Mar 1867	WI-Mw	TBV
Bef 1860	Christl, Maria			Peter Hartman	30 Sep 1860	WI-Mw	TBV
30 Aug 1867	Christl, Veronica	26 Nov 1864	006		1867		B
30 Aug 1867	Christl, Wilhelm	21 Dec 1865	030		4 Apr 1868	WI-Mw	B
30 Aug 1867	Rudrich, Theresia	20 Sep 1840	076	Joseph Christl			B
Abt 1869	Groeschl, Theresia	7 Feb 1848	109	Anton Broeckel	25 Aug 1923	WI-C	B
Abt 1889	Pimpl, Karl	25 Mar 1879			27 May 1946	MN-S	TBV
Abt 1889	Pimpl, Wendelin	26 Oct 1884			15 Sep 1961	MN-S	TBV
Kschiha / Čihaná							
31 Aug 1855	Leitner, Elizabeth	21 Mar 1837	36	Frank Wettstein	10 Mar 1905	WI-C	B
1 Sep 1855	Leitner, Engelbert	8 Oct 1836	15	Theresa Nadler	24 Mar 1916	WI-C	B
1 Sep 1855	Neubauer, Anna	25 May 1855	32				B
1 Sep 1855	Neubauer, Raymond	16 Sep 1821	23	Theresia Lodes	2 Jun 1885	WI-C	B
1 Sep 1855	Neubauer, Teresia	30 Aug 1852	32		28 May 1866	WI-FDL	B
21 Aug 1856	David, Anton	2 Feb 1855	28		27 Apr 1914	WI-Cl	B
21 Aug 1856	David, Michael	3 Oct 1849	28		29 Oct 1923	WI-C	B
21 Aug 1856	David, Wenzel	6 Jul 1819	35	Theresia Pichl	23 Dec 1910	WI-C	B
21 Aug 1856	*David, Wenzel	6 Jul 1819	35	Chatrina Bauer	23 Dec 1910	WI-C	B
21 Aug 1856	Egerer, Anna Maria	2 Sep 1803	22	Franz Anton Lenz	1879		B
21 Aug 1856	*Egerer, Anna Maria	2 Sep 1803	22	Norbert Kutzer	1879		B
21 Aug 1856	Hammer, Frank Joseph	15 Sep 1831	07	Franziska Schreck	1 Jul 1896	WI-C	B
21 Aug 1856	Pichl, Theresia	10 Sep 1814	15	Wenzel David	Bef 1860		B
21 Aug 1856	*Pichl, Theresia	10 Sep 1814	15	Norbert Leitner	Bef 1860		B
Bef 1864	Schmidt, Elizabeth	27 Jan 1845	31	Ferdinand Schott	1914	WI-C	B

15 Aug 1867	Hammer, Franziska	6 Jul 1837	07	Wendelin Miller	Bef 1880		B
23 May 1870	David, Raimund	1 Dec 1814	20	Anna Niemochl			B
23 May 1870	Lenz, Wenzel	3 Jun 1808	18	Barbara Hacker	16 Sep 1897	WI-C	B
Pfaffengrün / Popovice							
25 Aug 1906	Korn, Anton	27 Mar 1880	08				B
Rauschenbach / Sitiny							
14 Sep 1854	Nadler, Katharina	6 Nov 1816	26	Anton Pimpl	7 May 1891	WI-M	B
Bef 1864	Schmidt, John	5 Mar 1802	12	Franziska Wurtinger	15 Oct 1879	WI-Mw	B
Bef 1864	Wurtinger, Franziska	14 Feb 1815	29	John Schmidt	26 Apr 1891	WI-Mw	B
23 May 1870	David, Engelbert	15 May 1844	16		1 Mar 1899	MO	B
23 May 1870	David, Siard	25 Jul 1853	16		2 Dec 1906	MO	B
23 May 1870	David, Stephan	21 Mar 1847	16		1 Oct 1902	MO	B
23 May 1870	David, Wendelin	1 Dec 1848	16		5 Jan 1903	MO	B
23 May 1870	Niemochl, Anna	28 Jun 1821	16	Raimund David			B
PARISH - Habakladrau / Ovesne Kladruby							
Abaschin / Závišín							
31 Aug 1855	Broeckel, Anton	3 Dec 1845	02	Theresia Groeschl	12 Nov 1895	WI-C	B
31 Aug 1855	Denk, Anna Marie	21 Jan 1821	20	Anton Reinl	28 Mar 1894	WI-C	B
31 Aug 1855	Reinl, Anna	15 Jan 1854	02	Frank Joseph Nadler	13 May 1937	WI-C	B
31 Aug 1855	Reinl, Anna Mary	20 Dec 1841	20		7 Apr 1921	SD	B
31 Aug 1855	Reinl, Anton	9 Feb 1819	03	Anna Marie Denk	18 Nov 1893	WI-C	B
31 Aug 1855	Reinl, Elisabeth	23 Jan 1846	04	Anton Turba	16 Jul 1923	WI-C	B
31 Aug 1855	Reinl, Franz Joseph	11 Jul 1848	02	Katharina Lerch	21 Apr 1926	WI-S	B
31 Aug 1855	Reinl, Franziska	11 Sep 1851	02	Peter Keuler	6 Sep 1929	WI-C	B

Habakladrau / Ovesne Kladruby							
1 Sep 1855	Lodes, Anna	14 Nov 1804	24	Joseph Anton Rummer	21 May 1881		B
1 Sep 1855	Rummer, Joseph Anton	5 Feb 1807	07	Anna Lodes	27 Oct 1895		B
1 Sep 1855	Rummer, Margaretha	10 May 1842	68	Maximilian Hiederer	22 Dec 1925	WI-C	B
1 Sep 1855	Rummer, Maria	1 Nov 1843	68	Peter Lotzer	19 Dec 1872	WI-C	B
1 Sep 1855	Rummer, Theresia	20 May 1846	68	Anton Kocher	11 Jan 1937	WI-C	B
6 Aug 1856	Pop, Katharina	10 Nov 1788	33	Raimund Steiner			B
21 Aug 1856	Neubauer, Michael	24 Mar 1824	31				B
21 Aug 1856	Pop, Ferdinand	16 Feb 1840		Anna Kiesner	8 Jan 1923	WI-C	TBV
21 Aug 1856	Pop, John	20 Jun 1816	33	Katharina Weber	26 May 1892	WI-C	B
21 Aug 1856	Pop, Joseph	30 Dec 1841	33		2 Feb 1903	WI-C	B
21 Aug 1856	Pop, Theresa	3 May 1844	33	Ferdinand Lodes	30 Oct 1921	WI-C	B
21 Aug 1856	Rosner, Albert	10 Jul 1802	25	Anna Maria Turba			B
21 Aug 1856	Rosner, Engelbert	2 Mar 1838	25				B
21 Aug 1856	Schneider, Theresa	27 Mar 1809	30	Michael Turba	8 Aug 1893	WI-C	B
21 Aug 1856	Turba, Anton	27 Nov 1834	08	Elisabeth Reinl	8 Dec 1922	WI-C	B
21 Aug 1856	Turba, Frances	20 Dec 1842	08		30 Oct 1925	WI-C	B
21 Aug 1856	Turba, Mary Anna Theresa	16 Feb 1846	08	Joseph Michael Gubka	20 Jan 1919	SD	B
21 Aug 1856	Turba, Michael	5 Sep 1807	08	Theresa Schneider	14 Sep 1896	WI-C	B
21 Aug 1856	Turba, Theresa	26 Apr 1837	08		17 Sep 1923	WI-C	B
27 Sep 1856	Hanika, Herman Joseph	12 Jul 1829	32	Catherine Loesch	12 May 1927	NE	B
18 Jun 1868	Kogerer, Fransiska	1 Dec 1825	59	Joseph Rott	5 Jul 1891	WI-C	B
18 Jun 1868	Rott, Anton	22 May 1863	59	Anna Maria Wettstein	17 Jun 1940	WI-C	B
18 Jun 1868	*Rott, Anton	22 May 1863	59	Theresa Wettstein	17 Jun 1940	WI-C	B
18 Jun 1868	Rott, Franz Josef	27 Jan 1857	59	Elizabeth Kuehnl	13 Aug 1913	WI-C	B
18 Jun 1868	Rott, Joseph	6 Jan 1813	07	Fransiska Kogerer	1 Jan 1888	WI-C	B
12 Jun 1873	Lodes, Margaret Mary	28 Oct 1871			11 Dec 1958	IA-PA	B
30 Dec 1874	Lodes, Franz Josef	1 Oct 1872	36				B
30 Dec 1874	Lodes, Theresa	19 Jan 1866	36	Engelbert Miller	19 Feb 1952	WI-C	B
30 Dec 1874	Lodes, Wenzel	2 Mar 1807	24	Anna Maria Wurdinger	5 Dec 1890	WI-C	B
30 Dec 1874	*Lodes, Wenzel	2 Mar 1807	24	Anna Schusser	5 Dec 1890	WI-C	B

30 Dec 1874	Schusser, Anna	28 Jul 1815	51	Wenzel Lodes	15 Aug 1888	WI-C	B
Oct 1911	Hammer, Aegidius	3 Mar 1902			1 Jun 1944	WI-C	TBV
Oct 1911	Hammer, John	26 Nov 1903			19 Jan 1989	CA	TBV
Oct 1911	Hammer, Mary	26 Apr 1907			7 Jun 1986	WI-S	TBV
Oct 1911	Hammer, Richard	15 Jul 1910			7 Aug 1989	WI-C	TBV
Oct 1911	Kogerer, Albina	10 May 1873	55	Michael Hammer	14 Dec 1961	WI-C	B
26 Aug 1913	Degl, Frank	11 Sep 1891	61		8 Oct 1956		B
Bef 1954	Rott, Theresia	8 Jul 1926			Dec 2006	NY	TBV
Bef 1989	Steidl, Albert	27 Oct 1917	67		5 Aug 1989		B
Hohendorf / Zádub							
Abt 1882	Schusser, Joseph	8 Oct 1873	25		13 Nov 1939	WI-C	TBV
Müllestau / Milhostov							
Abt 1855	Wurtinger, Katharina	25 Feb 1814	13	Raimund Pimpl	22 Mar 1895	IA-S	B
18 Jun 1889	Windirsch, Mary	13 Sep 1845	01	Mathias Joseph Windirsch	21 Sep 1910	WI-C	B
18 Jun 1889	Windirsch, Mathias Joseph	20 Nov 1840	06	Mary Windirsch	Nov 1923	WI-C	B
18 Jun 1889	Windirsch, Therese	17 Oct 1867	01	Jacob Hansen	27 Jun 1940	WI-C	TBV
Abt 1894	Huttl, Franz Josef	13 Jan 1860	05	Maria Denk			MARR
Wischezahn / Vysočany							
6 Aug 1856	Schmidt, Franz J	15 Apr 1853	15				B
6 Aug 1856	Schmidt, Henry Englebert	14 Dec 1844		Frances Barbara Johnson	14 Apr 1929	WA	TBV
6 Aug 1856	Steiner, Adalbert	20 Oct 1815	15	Maria Anna Gintner	30 Nov 1906	WI-C	B
6 Aug 1856	Steiner, Anton	4 Nov 1842	10	Magdalena Bonlander	11 Jul 1909	WI-C	B
6 Aug 1856	Steiner, Frank Joseph	25 Oct 1851	10	Gertrude Franzen	30 May 1902	WI-C	B
6 Aug 1856	Steiner, Raimund	7 Oct 1789	15	Katharina Pop	16 Sep 1867	WI-FDL	B
6 Aug 1856	Steiner, Teresa	8 Sep 1848	10	John Daun	7 Jan 1918	WI-C	B
Jun 1869	Zepnick, Wenzel	24 Oct 1864	04		1937	WI-O	TBV

12 Jun 1873	Lodes, Anton Frederick	26 Dec 1866	14	Anna S Casper	1940	WI-WA	B
12 Jun 1873	*Lodes, Anton Frederick	26 Dec 1866	14	Mabel M Groff	1940	WI-WA	B
12 Jun 1873	Lodes, Frank Josef	30 May 1869			18 Feb 1930	CA	TBV
12 Jun 1873	Steiner, Anna	18 Jun 1846	14	Wenzel Lodes	25 Nov 1899	IA-PA	B
18 Apr 1955	Arbes, Eleonore	22 Apr 1921	13	Kurt G Eisen	25 Aug 2005	MN-B	TBV
Wischowitz / Výškovice							
6 Aug 1856	Gintner, Maria Anna	3 Dec 1820	15	Adalbert Steiner	22 Mar 1889	WI-C	B
7 Aug 1867	Nadler, Andreas	16 Nov 1832	12	Theresia Buchtinger	29 Aug 1913	WI-C	B
7 Aug 1867	Nadler, Josepha Sophia	8 Apr 1859	12		29 Jul 1939	WI-C	TBV
7 Aug 1867	Nadler, Theresia	22 Jun 1861	12		16 Mar 1887	WI-C	TBV
18 Jun 1868	Gintner, Frances Maria	25 Sep 1829	15	Herman Muller	27 Jan 1906	WI-C	B
18 Jun 1868	*Gintner, Frances Maria	25 Sep 1829	15	George Apfelbacher	27 Jan 1906	WI-C	B
Jun 1869	Zepnick, Anna	28 Apr 1862	04		29 Sep 1936	WI-OZ	TBV
Jun 1869	Zepnick, Franziska	23 Mar 1866	04		20 Mar 1928	WI-C	TBV
PARISH - Pistau / Pístov							
Martinau / Martinov							
6 Aug 1856	Hiederer, Anna	23 Nov 1836	03	Bartholmaeus Roeder	19 Mar 1922	WI-C	B
6 Aug 1856	Hiederer, Elisabeth	21 Nov 1845	03				B
6 Aug 1856	Hiederer, John Anton	6 May 1852	03		20 Jan 1929	OR	B
6 Aug 1856	Hiederer, Joseph Anton	8 Nov 1796	03	Anna Maria Pfrogler	1871		B
6 Aug 1856	Hiederer, Katerina	28 Oct 1794	03				B
6 Aug 1856	Hiederer, Maximilian	21 Apr 1834	01	Margaretha Rummer	7 Mar 1913	WI-C	B
6 Aug 1856	Hiederer, Theresia	5 Nov 1839	03	Jacob Kloetsch	12 May 1894	OR	B
6 Aug 1856	Pfrogler, Anna Maria	18 Nov 1809	01	Joseph Anton Hiederer	Sep 1894		B

Wilkowitz / Vlkovice							
1 Sep 1855	Schmiedl, Frances	1807		Lawrence Schott	Aft 1880		TBV
1 Sep 1855	Schott, Englebert	5 Nov 1844	22	Elizabeth Louise Neighbert	20 Jan 1905	OR	B
1 Sep 1855	Schott, Ferdinand	4 Jan 1841	22	Elizabeth Schmidt	1915	WI-C	B
1 Sep 1855	Schott, Lawrence	19 Nov 1802	12	Katharina Watzka			B
1 Sep 1855	*Schott, Lawrence	19 Nov 1802	12	Frances Schmiedl			B
6 Aug 1856	Schmidt, Elisabeth	18 Oct 1836	18	Theodore W Thommes	7 Jun 1917	MN-R	B
18 Jun 1868	Schicker, Anton	10 Jun 1808	07	Theresia Heidl	1885	WI-C	B
PARISH - Royau / Rájov							
Royau / Rájov							
Abt 1854	Rahmer, Franziska	14 Aug 1827	34	Raimund Egerer	2 Oct 1914	WI-C	B
14 Sep 1854	Egerer, Raimund	3 Jul 1826	13	Franziska Rahmer	1 Nov 1899	WI-C	B
14 Sep 1854	Fischbach, Barbora Anna	13 Apr 1823	23	Raymond Lenz	18 Oct 1886	SD	B
14 Sep 1854	Hammer, Marie Anna	6 Apr 1815	08	Raymund Lodes	22 Mar 1887	WI-C	B
14 Sep 1854	Lenz, Anna	20 Apr 1848	46	Jacob Klapperich	11 May 1942	SD	B
14 Sep 1854	Lenz, Franz Josef	24 Dec 1851	46		1854		B
14 Sep 1854	Lenz, Raymond	5 Dec 1823	46	Barbora Anna Fischbach	25 Dec 1911	SD	B
14 Sep 1854	Lodes, Anna	17 May 1851	08	Balthasar Pimpl	2 Feb 1940	WI-D	B
14 Sep 1854	Lodes, Ferdinand	20 May 1842	08	Theresa Pop	21 Jun 1907	WI-C	B
14 Sep 1854	Lodes, Francesca	19 Feb 1844	19		24 May 1920	WI-FDL	B
14 Sep 1854	Lodes, Mary Paschalis	14 Aug 1847	08		7 Feb 1879	IL	B
14 Sep 1854	Lodes, Raymund	30 Oct 1814	19	Marie Anna Hammer	28 Sep 1885	WI-C	B
14 Sep 1854	Lodes, Theresia	8 Dec 1837	08	August Nisler	13 Sep 1902	WI-C	B
14 Sep 1854	Pimpl, Anton	11 Jun 1809	03	Katharina Nadler	21 Jun 1871	WI-M	B
14 Sep 1854	Pimpl, Balthasar	4 Jan 1848	03	Anna Lodes	16 Aug 1919	WI-D	B
14 Sep 1854	Pimpl, Ferdinand	1 Oct 1811	72				B
14 Sep 1854	Pimpl, Ferdinand	14 Aug 1843	03	Louise Boehm	19 Jun 1913	WI-M	B
14 Sep 1854	Pimpl, Margaretha	7 Feb 1851	03				B

14 Sep 1854	Pimpl, Wendelin	26 Jun 1838	03		1892	WI-D	B
Abt 1855	Pimpl, Anna	14 Apr 1843	72	Lambert Hoffman	21 Sep 1916	IA-S	B
Abt 1855	Pimpl, Anton	12 Jan 1846	72		27 Dec 1866	WI-FDL	B
Abt 1855	Pimpl, Mauriz	16 Oct 1850	72		2 Jul 1924	IA-S	B
Abt 1855	Pimpl, Theresia	29 Sep 1849	72				B
Abt 1855	Pimpl, Wendelin	23 Jul 1852	72	Theresa Isoff	13 Oct 1946	WI-B	B
Jul 1855	Pimpl, Raimund	5 Dec 1814	72	Katharina Wurtinger	21 Oct 1875	IA-S	B
Jul 1855	*Pimpl, Raimund	5 Dec 1814	72	Teresia Pimpl	21 Oct 1875	IA-S	B
31 Aug 1855	Egerer, Theresia	25 Nov 1829	37	Bernhard Seichter	18 Oct 1905	WI-C	B
31 Aug 1855	Fischer, Engelbert	3 Mar 1853	27				B
31 Aug 1855	Fischer, Ferdinand	6 Aug 1848	27	Theresa Lenz	1920	WI-C	B
31 Aug 1855	Fischer, Joseph	6 Mar 1825	08	Maria Anna Nadler	Aft 1900	WI-C	B
31 Aug 1855	Kutzer, Anton	3 Jan 1835	46	Elizabeth Faulk	3 Jun 1900	ND	B
31 Aug 1855	Kutzer, Barbara	23 Jan 1840	46				B
31 Aug 1855	Nadler, Frank Joseph	15 Aug 1853	70	Anna Reinl	29 Sep 1934	WI-C	B
31 Aug 1855	Nadler, Franz Joseph	15 Oct 1816	66	Anna Reinl	20 Nov 1894	WI-C	B
31 Aug 1855	Nadler, Johann	27 Feb 1851	55		11 Jun 1862	WI-FDL	B
31 Aug 1855	Nadler, Maria Anna	23 Feb 1819	66	Joseph Fischer	9 Jun 1903	WI-C	B
31 Aug 1855	Schierl, Franziska	10 Mar 1835	25	John Peter Kriescher	1871		B
1 Sep 1855	Leitner, Ann	22 May 1851	52		1 Feb 1924	WI-C	B
1 Sep 1855	Leitner, Frank	15 Oct 1853	52	Christine Wick	15 Dec 1910	WI-C	B
1 Sep 1855	Leitner, Theresa	13 Nov 1828	52	Engelbert Popp			B
1 Sep 1855	Leitner, Wenzel	5 Oct 1821	52	Barbora Popp	28 Apr 1890	WI-C	B
1 Sep 1855	Leitner, Wihelmine	1855			Bef 1860		TBV
1 Sep 1855	Lodes, Theresia	11 Nov 1820	19	Raymond Neubauer	2 Sep 1889	WI-C	B
1 Sep 1855	Popp, Barbora	8 Oct 1825	47	Wenzel Leitner	2 Apr 1899	WI-C	B
1 Sep 1855	*Popp, Barbora	8 Oct 1825	47		2 Apr 1899	WI-C	B
1 Sep 1855	Popp, Engelbert	21 Jul 1830	06	Theresa Leitner			B
1 Sep 1855	Popp, Theresa	21 Oct 1843	06				B
Abt 1856	Lenz, Barbara	26 Dec 1838	67				B
Abt 1856	Lenz, Engelbart	5 Feb 1813	40	Franziska Schierl	24 Nov 1893	WI-C	B
Abt 1856	Lenz, Ferdinand	8 Jan 1850	67		12 Nov 1925	WI-C	B

Abt 1856	Schierl, Franziska	26 Apr 1812	67	Engelbart Lenz	1877	WI-C	B
Abt 1856	Schierl, Johann	4 Apr 1835	67	Rosina Hohnberger	May 1929	WI-WIN	B
21 Aug 1856	Hammer, Engelbert	27 Oct 1855	36				B
21 Aug 1856	Kutzer, Anna	5 Jan 1851	04	Carl Wettstein	16 Jun 1923	WI-C	B
21 Aug 1856	Kutzer, Norbert	26 Jun 1803	04	Anna Maria Egerer	5 Apr 1894		B
21 Aug 1856	Leitner, Johann Martin	11 Apr 1791	52	Margaritha Denk	1868	WI-C	B
21 Aug 1856	Lenz, Franz Josef	8 Jan 1841	54		1889		B
21 Aug 1856	Lenz, Theresia	22 Jan 1818	40				B
21 Aug 1856	Schreck, Franziska	1 Mar 1835	36	Frank Joseph Hammer	19 Mar 1917	WI-C	B
21 Aug 1856	Turba, Anna Maria	16 Jun 1809	68	Albert Rosner			B
15 Aug 1867	Miller, Engelbert	14 Oct 1862	36	Theresa Lodes	9 Jul 1922	WI-C	B
15 Aug 1867	Miller, Theresa	8 Feb 1861	36				B
15 Aug 1867	Miller, Wendall	12 Nov 1865	32		27 Mar 1912	WI-C	B
15 Aug 1867	Miller, Wendelin	10 Jun 1838	32	Anna Lodes	20 Jul 1914	WI-C	B
15 Aug 1867	*Miller, Wendelin	10 Jun 1838	32	Franziska Hammer	20 Jul 1914	WI-C	B
7 Dec 1868	Lenz, Theresa	23 Jul 1851	53	Ferdinand Fischer	1934	WI-C	B
7 Dec 1868	Turba, Anna	15 Dec 1848	68				B
Bef 1870	Lenz, Anton	15 May 1849	53				B
23 May 1870	David, Moriz	26 Feb 1861	72		20 Mar 1909	MO	B
23 May 1870	David, Theresia	14 Sep 1858	72		16 Jun 1948	MO	B
23 May 1870	Lenz, Lambert	17 Sep 1853	74		10 Sep 1889	MN-N	B
23 May 1870	Lenz, Raymond	27 Mar 1844	53		1927	WI-C	B
23 May 1870	Lenz, Wenzel	27 Sep 1846	53				B
16 Jun 1870	Cardinal, Theresia	18 Jan 1821	50	Lorenz Zitterbart			B
Abt 1882	Rahma, Theresa	25 Nov 1829	34	Ferdinand Schusser	6 May 1887	WI-C	B
22 May 1882	Egerer, Franz Anton	15 Dec 1823	13		15 Jan 1883	WI-C	B
22 May 1882	Egerer, Maria	5 Mar 1841	13	Raimund Schierl	11 Aug 1915	WI-C	B
22 May 1882	*Egerer, Maria	5 Mar 1841	13	Josef Meisel	11 Aug 1915	WI-C	B
22 May 1882	Schierl, Wendelin	2 Jun 1871	13		19 Aug 1958	WI-C	B
Abt 1889	Pimpl, Wendelin	11 Jul 1851	26	Anna Rosch	7 Mar 1920	MN-S	B
11 Nov 1908	Pimpl, Johann	15 Jul 1882	08				B

PARISH - Tepl Stadt / Teplá-město							
Böhmisch Borau / Beranov							
21 Aug 1856	Weber, Katharina	26 Feb 1815	16	John Pop	11 Nov 1866	WI-FDL	B
Enkengrün / Jankovice							
Abt 1855	Kocherer, Frank Joseph	8 Nov 1849	18	Josephine Hoffmann	15 Jun 1908	WI-Cl	B
Abt 1855	Kogerer, Franz	25 Jul 1819	18	Margaretha Wanka			B
Abt 1855	Kogerer, Jacob	1843					TBV
Abt 1855	Kogerer, Josepha	15 Apr 1836	18				B
Abt 1855	Kogerer, Josephine	11 Mar 1854	18				B
Abt 1855	Kogerer, Theresa	5 Oct 1847	18				B
Abt 1855	Wanka, Margaretha	5 Jan 1822	12	Franz Kogerer			B
31 Aug 1855	Kocher, Anton	14 Dec 1830	18	Theresia Rummer	15 Apr 1907	WI-C	B
23 May 1870	Hohler, Franz Josef	19 Mar 1822	24	Katharina Egerer			B
Lusading / Služetín							
31 Aug 1855	Nadler, Theresa	30 Jan 1845	24	Engelbert Leitner	31 Jul 1935	WI-C	B
31 Aug 1855	Reinl, Anna	3 May 1819	24	Franz Joseph Nadler	12 Mar 1891	WI-C	B
23 May 1870	Egerer, Katharina	24 Nov 1826	21	Franz Josef Hohler			B
23 May 1870	Hohler, Franz	1 Jan 1863	21				B
23 May 1870	Hohler, Josef	2 Aug 1853	21		11 Aug 1926	MO	B
22 May 1882	Riedl, Anna	6 Jul 1837	05	Adolph Kuehnl	25 Jan 1914	WI-C	B
5 May 1953	Weber, Maria	3 Feb 1925	04				TBV
Pauten / Poutnov							
21 Aug 1856	Fischer, Catherine	5 Jan 1839	37	Frank Unger	31 Dec 1873	NY	B
21 Aug 1856	Fischer, Engelbert	5 May 1846	37				B

21 Aug 1856	Fischer, Vincent	8 Feb 1813	37	Frances Hohler	14 Jul 1890		B
16 Jun 1870	Zitterbart, Lorenz	24 Oct 1816	05	Theresia Cardinal			B
Pobitz / Babice							
7 Dec 1868	Lenz, Anna	27 Feb 1840	14				B
23 May 1870	Hacker, Barbara	3 Mar 1817	14	Wenzel Lenz	26 Apr 1884	WI-C	B
Tepl Stadt / Teplá-město							
Abt 1878	Ertl, Barbara	16 Aug 1863	078		1940	NE	B
Abt 1883	Ertl, Bertha	7 Mar 1876	078		19 Jun 1925	NE	B
Abt 1884	Ertl, Louis Josef	22 Aug 1871	078		7 Nov 1960	NE	B
14 Nov 1895	Ertl, Aloisa	25 Dec 1878	234				B
Bef 1896	Ertl, Joseph	28 Sep 1839	078	Franziska Kraus	23 Dec 1896	NE	B
21 Apr 1900	Ertl, Hedwig	17 Oct 1877	234				B
21 Apr 1900	Ertl, Heinrich	26 Jul 1885	234		7 Aug 1939	NY	B
Special Designations:				**Months:**			
Abt = About				01 = Jan = January			
Aft = After				02 = Feb = February			
Bef = Before				03 = Mar = March			
*Name = Multiple marriages				04 = Apr = April			
**Name = Multiple trips to the United States				05 = May = May			
				06 = Jun = June			
				07 = Jul = July			
Record Types:				08 = Aug = August			
B = Baptismal and/or Christening Record				09 = Sep = September			
MARR = Marriage Record				10 = Oct = October			
TBV = To Be Verified				11 = Nov = November			
				12 = Dec = December			

The Wave of Emigration Beginning in 1850 from Tepla Land, Bohemia
and Surrounding Areas to Calumet County, Wisconsin
- Other Findings

Arrival in U.S.A.	Name	Born/Baptised	House No.	Spouse	Died	Burial	Record Types
PARISH - Albersdörfer Brand / Miliře							
Girnbert / Zadni Miliře							
Jun 1868	Schiffl, Maria Anna	4 Feb 1822	03	Michael Zeidler	12 Apr 1886	WI-M	B
Jun 1868	Zeidler, Frank William	31 Aug 1847	14	Wilhelmina Tesch	26 Feb 1916	WI-M	B
Jun 1868	Zeidler, Michael	1 Jan 1821	14	Maria Anna Schiffl	24 Jun 1894	WI-M	B
22 May 1873	Letz, Catharine	4 Jan 1864	15		16 May 1952	WI-M	B
22 May 1873	Letz, Maria	10 Oct 1870	15		4 May 1931	WI-M	B
22 May 1873	Zeidler, Anna	20 Dec 1842	03	John Adam Letz	5 May 1930	WI-M	B
PARISH - Auherzen / Úherce							
Auherzen / Úherce							
31 Jul 1868	Schaffer, Andreas	25 Jan 1828	09	Anna Feyerfeil	21 Apr 1910	WI-Mw	B
Blattnitz / Blatnice							
Abt 1861	Plutz, Joseph	22 Nov 1841	03	Maria Barbara Seidel	21 Mar 1911	WI-BR	B
12 Sep 1863	Felber, Anton	22 Apr 1853	03		1903	WI-Mw	B
12 Sep 1863	Felber, Mathias	Mar 1828		Maria Plutz	16 Jun 1905	WI-Mw	MARR
12 Sep 1863	Plutz, Maria	23 Oct 1829	03	Mathias Felber	29 Jan 1903	WI-Mw	B
6 Jul 1868	Faber, Barbara	1836		Johann Plutz	1930	WI-DR	MARR

6 Jul 1868	*Faber, Barbara	1836		Anton Petrasek	1930	WI-DR	MARR
6 Jul 1868	Plutz, Elisabeth	17 Jun 1865	27		1 May 1931		B
6 Jul 1868	Plutz, Johann	3 Aug 1836	03	Barbara Faber	1926	WI-DR	B
6 Jul 1868	Plutz, Johann	6 Sep 1867	27		18 Apr 1931		B
6 Jul 1868	Plutz, Margaretha	11 Dec 1847	03		3 Jun 1927	WI-J	B
Nürschan / Nýřany							
Bef 1962	Helgert, Aloysia	11 Oct 1886	10	Franz Kubicek	4 Jan 1962	WI-M	B
PARISH - Auschowitz / Úšovice							
Auschowitz / Úšovice							
4 Nov 1856	Ries, Catherine	23 Feb 1819	37	Joseph Heimerl	18 Jul 1892	WI-FDL	B
18 Jun 1868	Muller, Sigmund	14 Jul 1854	51	Annie Koehler	20 Mar 1933	WI-C	B
15 Jun 1910	**Muller, Sigmund	14 Jul 1854	51	Annie Koehler	20 Mar 1933	WI-C	B
26 May 1952	Eisen, Helmut Gustav	2 Mar 1923			11 Jul 2001	MN-H	TBV
18 Apr 1955	Eisen, Kurt G	27 Aug 1921		Eleonore Arbes	18 Aug 2001	MN-B	TBV
PARISH - Bleistadt / Oloví							
Horn / Hory							
7 May 1880	Nickasch, Anton	10 Dec 1862	32	Margaretha Marie Wettengel	23 Feb 1949	WI-O	B
23 Oct 1884	Nickasch, Andrew	18 Jan 1838	32	Margaret Krause	1888	WI-O	B
23 Oct 1884	Nickasch, Joseph	9 Jun 1870	32		24 Nov 1950	WI-O	B
PARISH - Chlum Svate Mari / Chlum Svaté Maří							
Boden / Boden							

9 Aug 1881	Deissler, Maria Magdalena	29 Apr 1820	38	Georg Michael Vogl	9 Nov 1885	WI-M	B
Chlum Svate Mari / Chlum Svaté Maří							
Bef 1854	Riedl, Charles	21 Sep 1845	76				B
Bef 1854	Riedl, John	16 Oct 1805	76	Marie Anna Fischer	6 Feb 1880	MA	B
Bef 1854	Riedl, John J	9 Aug 1835	76		27 Feb 1899	MA	B
Bef 1854	Riedl, Joseph	8 Apr 1838	65		8 Jun 1923	MA	B
Bef 1854	Riedl, Mary	16 Feb 1840	76		20 Apr 1907	MA	B
Bef 1854	Riedl, Matthew	16 Oct 1842	76		Jan 1876	MA	B
Bef 1854	Riedl, Michael	20 Mar 1833	76		4 Mar 1908	MA	B
Bef 1860	Riedl, Catherine Helen	17 Jun 1850	76	Fidelis Zitterbart	28 Dec 1913	PA	B
Bef 1860	Riedl, Madeline	11 Jan 1848	76		23 Jan 1881	MA	B
Daßnitz / Dasnice							
Bef 1854	Fischer, Marie Anna	30 Apr 1810	03	John Riedl	24 Jun 1891	MA	B
Kloben / Hlavno							
18 Nov 1867	Muehlhans, Andreas	16 Feb 1809	34	Marie Katherine Hetzer	9 Mar 1876		B
18 Nov 1867	Muehlhans, Andrew	11 Aug 1838	34		24 Dec 1905		B
18 Nov 1867	Muehlhans, Anton	11 Jun 1847	34				B
18 Nov 1867	Muehlhans, Catherina	5 Jan 1858	34				B
18 Nov 1867	Muehlhans, Charles	15 Mar 1850	34	Agnes Loeb			B
18 Nov 1867	Muehlhans, Frank	1 Oct 1852	34		4 Mar 1907		B
18 Nov 1867	Muehlhans, Wenzel	15 Mar 1850	34		5 Aug 1911	WI-M	B
23 Nov 1867	Vogl, Johann	16 Mar 1847	03		22 Feb 1907	WI-M	B
Abt 1880	Vogl, Magdaene Margareth	23 Feb 1844	03		25 Aug 1921	WI-M	B
Oct 1880	Vogl, Andreas	18 May 1859	37		10 Aug 1909	WI-M	B
9 Aug 1881	Kuhnl, Anna	5 Dec 1849		Johann Vogl	24 Jan 1920	WI-Mar	B
9 Aug 1881	Vogl, Christof	9 Feb 1852	37	Cecelia Hutter	1922	WI-Mar	B

9 Aug 1881	Vogl, Johann	27 Feb 1842	03	Anna Kuhnl	8 Feb 1916	WI-Mar	B
9 Aug 1881	Vogl, Margareth	28 Sep 1856	37		5 Feb 1946	WI-M	B
9 Aug 1881	Vogl, Margarette	23 May 1881	37				B
9 Aug 1881	Vogl, Theresia	12 Jul 1861	37		8 Feb 1931		B
PARISH - Chodau / Chodov							
Chodau / Chodov							
1 Sep 1855	Fischer, Anton	4 Feb 1800	08	Karolina Schwartl	1884		B
1 Sep 1855	Fischer, Anton	27 Apr 1840			11 Oct 1917		TBV
1 Sep 1855	Fischer, Barbara	12 May 1842	74		1876		B
1 Sep 1855	Fischer, Franz Karl	3 Jul 1837	74		9 Jul 1887	WI-O	B
1 Sep 1855	Schwartl, Karolina	13 May 1800		Anton Fischer	27 Oct 1845		MARR
Bef 1860	Fischer, Anna	18 Aug 1824		Joseph Anton Stoehr	7 Jun 1897	WI-SH	MARR
Bef 1926	Fischer, Franziska	3 Apr 1831	74		1926		B
PARISH - Donawitz / Stanovice							
Trossau / Dražov							
27 May 1867	Breitfelder, Ferdinand	2 Feb 1834	01	Francizisca Keilberth	6 Dec 1895	IN	B
27 May 1867	Breitfelder, Franz Joseph	25 Feb 1836	01		26 May 1911	OH	B
PARISH - Elbogen / Loket							
Grünlas / Loučky							
Abt 1855	Stoehr, Joseph Anton	20 Jun 1818	24	Anna Fischer	11 Dec 1888	WI-SH	B
Bef 1860	Stoehr, Wenzel	20 Mar 1848	24	Margareth Heckel	27 Feb 1914	WI-SH	B

PARISH - Falkenau / Sokolov							
Zwodau / Svatana							
9 Aug 1881	Vogl, Anne	19 Jan 1879	82		1897		B
PARISH - Frohnau / Vranov							
Ebmeth / Rovná							
Bef 1856	Weiss, Albert	18 Feb 1846	21		3 Apr 1924	WI-O	B
Bef 1856	Weiss, Erwin Joseph	14 Mar 1853	21				B
Bef 1856	Weiss, Franz Anton	3 Jan 1811		Francisca Renz	22 Sep 1897	WI-O	B
Bef 1856	Weiss, Theresa	10 Apr 1842	21				B
Bef 1870	Weiss, Crescentia	24 Mar 1808	38	Joseph Anton Dorschner	27 Aug 1895	WI-O	B
15 Oct 1921	Theisinger, Marie Elizabeth	20 Dec 1898		Joseph Muehlhans	14 Dec 1943	WI-Mw	TBV
Frohnau / Vranov							
22 May 1882	Kuehnl, Adolph	18 Dec 1836	54	Anna Riedl	1912	WI-C	B
PARISH - Girsh / Krsy							
Geischowitz / Kejšovice							
Bef 1868	Gubka, Theresa	2 Nov 1844		Wenzel Koehler	2 Sep 1912	WI-C	TBV
7 Dec 1868	Gubka, Barbara	27 Mar 1852			26 Nov 1901	SD	TBV
7 Dec 1868	Gubka, Katherine	12 Jul 1842			27 Mar 1928	WI-C	TBV
Bef 1870	Blur, Anna Maria	1812		Andreas Gubka	2 Feb 1890	WI-C	TBV
Bef 1870	Gubka, Andreas	26 Oct 1796	17	Anna Maria Blur	12 May 1870	WI-C	B
Bef 1880	Gubka, Carl	Apr 1847			4 Mar 1926	MN-TR	TBV

Girsh / Krsy							
Jun 1869	Zepnick, Joseph	6 Jun 1838	31	Maria Anna Holtschick	19 Jun 1919	WI-C	B
PARISH - Gossengrün / Krajková							
Plumberg / Květná							
8 Sep 1873	Doerfner, Magdelina	24 Jun 1827	15	Andreas Wettengel	21 Jan 1878	WI-O	B
PARISH - Graslitz / Kraslice							
Graslitz / Kraslice							
2 Jul 1853	Enders, Theresa Marie	20 May 1827	012	Frederick Staniek	21 May 1900	PA	B
2 Jul 1853	Staniek, Andrew	24 May 1852	035				B
2 Jul 1853	Staniek, Frank	25 Oct 1848	012		16 Oct 1907	PA	B
2 Jul 1853	Staniek, Frederick	10 Aug 1822	204	Theresa Marie Enders	28 Feb 1875	PA	B
2 Jul 1853	Staniek, Joseph Enders	4 Feb 1847	627		4 Apr 1917	PA	B
Schönwerth / Krásná							
12 Oct 1853	Richter, Elisabetha	1815		Johann Wenzl Riedl	Oct 1853		TBV
12 Oct 1853	Riedl, Anna Maria	27 Aug 1832	05		29 Sep 1921		B
12 Oct 1853	Riedl, Eduard Christoph	10 May 1844	05		14 Mar 1890		B
12 Oct 1853	Riedl, Elisabetha	14 Jan 1837	05		29 Jul 1915		B
12 Oct 1853	Riedl, Franzika	11 Nov 1847	05		25 Jun 1934		B
12 Oct 1853	Riedl, Johann Wenzl	12 Feb 1805	06	Elisabetha Richter	Oct 1853		B
12 Oct 1853	Riedl, Johann Wenzl	9 Oct 1841	05		1867		B
12 Oct 1853	Riedl, Maria Magdalena	3 Dec 1834	05		5 Jan 1901		B

PARISH - Habersbirk / Habartov							
Meierhöfen / Dvory							
18 Nov 1867	Hetzer, Marie Katherine	10 Mar 1814	01	Andreas Muehlhans	18 Jul 1881		B
PARISH - Heiligenkreuz / Chodský Újezd							
Glasau / Neblažov							
1 Jun 1874	Gebhart, Adam	11 Apr 1868			4 Nov 1952	ND	TBV
1 Jun 1874	Gebhart, Andrew	25 Aug 1862		Anna Olrich	1922	WI-C	TBV
1 Jun 1874	Gebhart, Michael	31 Aug 1865			23 Nov 1941	MN-WL	TBV
1 Jun 1874	Gebhart, Wenzel	30 Dec 1827	01	Katharina Seidler	12 Jul 1901	ND	B
18 Jun 1868	Gebhart, Margaret	3 Mar 1825	01	Johann Suttner	30 Aug 1881	WI-C	B
Heiligenkreuz / Chodský Újezd							
22 Jul 1922	Wenig, Wenzel	4 May 1895	53	Louise Rott	4 Feb 1980	WI-C	B
PARISH - Hohen - Zetlisch / Vysoké Sedliště							
Thein / Týnec							
23 Apr 1893	Friedl, Michael	10 Aug 1873	22	Margareta Hederer	25 May 1939	WI-R	B
Abt 1895	Friedl, Margaret	21 Apr 1877	22	Frank Aloysius Schimanski	24 Oct 1970	WI-R	B
Abt 1895	Friedl, Mary	21 Oct 1879	22	John Goeser	1 Apr 1956	WI-C	B
10 May 1895	Friedl, Anna	7 Jun 1882	22		20 Mar 1929	WI-R	B
10 May 1895	Friedl, Joseph	30 Mar 1884	22		1941		B
10 May 1895	Friedl, Matthias	20 Sep 1841	22	Maria Anna Hoerl	18 Apr 1925	WI-R	B
10 May 1895	Friedl, Theresa	27 Apr 1889	22	Frank Schneider	21 Nov 1922	WI-C	B
10 May 1895	Hoerl, Maria Anna	30 May 1849	06	Matthias Friedl	4 Jun 1928	WI-R	B

2 Jul 1896	Hoerl, Anna	27 Dec 1881	06				B
2 Jul 1896	Hoerl, Fredrick	10 Jan 1889	06		5 Jul 1978	WI-M	B
2 Jul 1896	Hoerl, Margaretha	21 Feb 1891	06				B
2 Jul 1896	Hoerl, Maria	22 Jun 1877	06	Anton E Kuehnl	1949	WI-C	B
2 Jul 1896	Hoerl, Marie	4 Apr 1862	06				B
2 Jul 1896	Hoerl, Michael	29 Jun 1851	06	Margaret Holleck	1896	WI-C	B
2 Jul 1896	Hoerl, Michael	27 Nov 1883	06		15 Apr 1963	WI-C	B
2 Jul 1896	Hoerl, Sigmund	9 Sep 1885	06		5 Jan 1955	WI-S	B
2 Jul 1896	Hoerl, Wenzel	29 Jul 1892	06	Angeline Daun	13 Jun 1959	WI-C	TBV
2 Jul 1896	Holleck, Margaret	20 Dec 1851	18	Michael Hoerl	7 Mar 1930	WI-C	B
PARISH - Kapsch / Skapce							
Guratin / Krtín							
Abt 1855	Eigenberger, Joseph	15 May 1824	11	Maria Werthan	4 Nov 1888	IA-D	B
3 Sep 1855	Eigenberger, Maria	24 Mar 1830	11	Peter Sprenger	16 Jul 1884		B
PARISH - Kirchenbirk / Kostelni Briza							
Ruditzgrün / Rudolec							
22 May 1882	Kuehnl, Anton E	11 Jan 1872	20	Maria Hoerl	21 Jun 1940	WI-C	B
22 May 1882	Kuehnl, Elizabeth	20 May 1864	20	Franz Josef Rott	3 May 1920	WI-C	B
22 May 1882	Kuehnl, George	17 Aug 1878			6 Apr 1928	WI-C	TBV
22 May 1882	Kuehnl, Rose	10 Dec 1880		Michael Satzer	1939	WI-C	TBV
22 May 1882	Kuehnl, Wenzel	10 May 1869	20		1925	MN-S	B
PARISH - Königsberg / Kynšperk nad Ohři							
Golddorf / Zlatá							

27 May 1903	Muehlhans, Joseph	1 Feb 1879		Marie Elizabeth Theisinger	6 Jun 1959	WI-Mw	TBV
Krainhof / Dvorečky							
27 May 1867	Keilberth, Francizisca	7 Apr 1843	16	Ferdinand Breitfelder	22 Jun 1923	CA	B
PARISH - Kosolup / Kozolupy							
Kosolup / Kozolupy							
31 Jul 1868	Feyerfeil, Anna	2 Jul 1836	29	Andreas Schaffer	12 Jul 1909	WI-Mw	B
31 Jul 1868	Schaffer, Anna	8 Aug 1861	29				B
31 Jul 1868	Schaffer, Catherine	8 Jan 1857	29				B
31 Jul 1868	Schaffer, Elisabeth	26 Feb 1868	07		1956	WI-BR	B
31 Jul 1868	Schaffer, Joseph	12 Dec 1855	29		19 Oct 1909	MN-C	B
31 Jul 1868	Schaffer, Mary	16 Jun 1863	29				B
31 Jul 1868	Schaffer, Theresa	9 May 1860	29		13 Jan 1881	WI-Mw	B
31 Jul 1868	Schaffer, Wenzel	7 Apr 1858	29		1948	WI-BR	B
PARISH - Kostelzen / Kostelec							
Kostelzen / Kostelec							
Jun 1854	Franta, Barbara	7 Feb 1813	22	Adalbert Steiner	1 Apr 1899	WI-Mw	B
Jun 1854	Steiner, Adalbert	8 Oct 1810	07	Barbara Franta	24 Feb 1890	WI-Mw	B
Jun 1854	Steiner, Anna	31 Dec 1844	30	John Kulnick	27 Mar 1932	WI-Mw	B
Jun 1854	Steiner, Barbara	20 Jul 1848	30	Carl Forster	26 Jan 1910	MN-B	B
Jun 1854	Steiner, John	16 Sep 1841	30		1914	WI-Mw	B
Abt 1855	Ganka, Anna	31 Jul 1800	10	Johann Andreas Eigenberger	1855		B
Abt 1855	*Ganka, Anna	31 Jul 1800	10	Joseph Schiller	1855		B
5 Jun 1867	Dobner, Margareta	27 Oct 1843	01	Joseph Seifert	3 Nov 1916	MN-B	B

PARISH - Kumerau / Komárov							
Lohof / Lohov							
1 Sep 1855	Fuhr, Frances	7 Oct 1812	21	Joseph Wettstein	30 Mar 1873	WI-C	B
1 Sep 1855	Wettstein, Theresa	31 Dec 1834	21	Peter Joseph Keuler	23 May 1901	WI-C	B
PARISH - Landek / Otročín							
Landek / Otročín							
21 Aug 1856	Hohler, Frances	14 Dec 1811	18	Vincent Fischer	13 Nov 1896		B
Poschitz / Poseč							
Abt 1868	Heidl, Frank Joseph	7 Jan 1850	04		1921	NJ	B
PARISH - Lanz / Lomnice							
Pichelberg / Boučí							
23 Oct 1884	Krause, Margaret	7 Jun 1839	54	Andrew Nickasch	23 Apr 1915	WI-O	B
Thein / Týn							
8 Sep 1873	Wettengel, Andreas	11 Sep 1824	22	Magdelina Doerfner	1 May 1904	WI-O	B
8 Sep 1873	Wettengel, Katie	8 Apr 1857	22		20 Feb 1940	WI-O	B
8 Sep 1873	Wettengel, Margaretha Marie	29 Sep 1854	22	Anton Nickasch	9 Nov 1933	WI-O	B
Unter Negrün / Dolní Nivy							
9 Aug 1881	Hutter, Cecelia	9 Jul 1855	28	Christof Vogl	1891	WI-Mar	B

PARISH - Leskau / Lestkov							
Hohen Jamny / Vysoké Jamné							
Abt 1877	Hierath, Anna Lydia	3 May 1875	05		25 Dec 1954	ND	B
Abt 1877	Hierath, John Francis	4 Aug 1872	37		1928	ND	B
Abt 1877	Hierath, Joseph Karl	7 Nov 1847	12	Anna Marie Riedl	17 Apr 1918	CAN	B
Abt 1877	Riedl, Anna Marie	19 Aug 1846	03	Joseph Karl Hierath	14 Sep 1891	ND	B
Honau / Hanov							
Abt 1886	Benedickt, Josephine	19 Dec 1853	01	Karl Benedickt	5 Mar 1916	IA-HR	B
Kurschin / Kořen							
1 Jun 1874	Gebhart, Catharina	20 Feb 1874	46		16 Oct 1951	ND	B
27 Dec 1891	Patz, Anton	27 May 1855	05	Anna Tischler		OH	B
Leskau / Lestkov							
27 Sep 1856	Loesch, Catherine	20 Aug 1835	101	Herman Joseph Hanika	22 Jan 1905	NE	B
31 May 1882	Lotter, Theresa N	7 Aug 1865	109		29 Jan 1948	NE	B
23 Jun 1882	Loesch, John	4 Dec 1854	081		11 Sep 1920	NE	B
Abt 1885	Benedickt, Karl	1 Aug 1854	041	Josephine Benedickt	18 Feb 1932	IA-HR	B
Abt 1886	Benedickt, Joseph John	6 Apr 1883	041		11 Jan 1957	NE	B
Abt 1886	Benedickt, Rose Margaret	8 Mar 1878	041		16 Aug 1963	IA-HR	B
8 Nov 1888	Lotter, Julie Sophie	20 Oct 1870	050		25 May 1952	KS	B
Jul 1895	Loesch, Anna	13 Jan 1839	109	Josef Lotter	25 Sep 1922		B
Jul 1895	Lotter, Anna	4 Aug 1872	050		28 Apr 1946	NE	B
Jul 1895	Lotter, Emilie	11 Jun 1874	050		2 Jan 1947	NE	B
Bef 1900	Lotter, Frank	7 Jan 1867	109				B

PARISH - Lobs / Lobzy							
Steinbach / Kamenice							
Bef 1864	Dorschner, Franz Karl	11 Jul 1846	54		31 Aug 1929	WI-O	B
Bef 1870	Dorschner, Joseph Anton	31 May 1810	54	Crescentia Weiss	21 Dec 1870	WI-O	B
Bef 1880	Dorschner, Anton	11 Dec 1834	54	Catherine Ebert	10 Apr 1903	WI-O	B
Bef 1906	Dorschner, Franz Anton	4 Jan 1849	54		28 Mar 1906	WI-O	B
Bef 1909	Dorschner, Franz	5 May 1837	54		23 Mar 1909	WI-O	B
Bef 1922	Dorschner, Joseph	27 Apr 1843	54		24 Mar 1922	WI-O	B
PARISH - Marienbad / Mariánské Lázně							
Marienbad / Mariánské Lázně							
Abt 1853	Utschig, Johann Nepomuk	11 Sep 1848	57	Catherine Rheude	29 Apr 1926	CA	B
29 Oct 1853	Utschig, Adolph	15 Nov 1837	44		16 Jan 1912	CA	B
29 Oct 1853	Utschig, Elisabetha	12 Oct 1835	44				B
29 Oct 1853	Utschig, Johanna	24 Mar 1830	15				B
Abt 1854	Utschig, Amelia	20 Apr 1832	15	Louis Spuller	13 May 1924		B
Abt 1854	*Utschig, Amelia	20 Apr 1832	15	Charles Brown	13 May 1924		B
17 Aug 1854	Cech, Amelia	1 Feb 1854	67				B
17 Aug 1854	Utschig, Anna	1 Sep 1828	15	Vincenz Cech			B
Bef 1876	Utschig, Ludwig	27 Jun 1845	57		5 Feb 1876	CA	B
10 Feb 1882	Popp, Johann Michael	14 Nov 1857	14		Bef 1910		B
PARISH - Neudek / Nejdek							
Bernau / Bernov							
Abt 1867	Schreiber, Martin	21 Oct 1833	138	Augusta Wilhelmine Heinz	2 Aug 1884	WI-SH	B

PARISH - Neudorf / Nová Ves							
Neudorf / Nová Ves							
8 Jul 1872	Reichl, Margaretha	20 May 1854	66		28 Apr 1913		B
31 Jul 1875	Reichl, George	20 May 1859	66		27 Aug 1889	IL	B
8 May 1878	Bauer, Katharina	13 Mar 1835	42	Wenzl Reichl	17 Dec 1907	IL	B
8 May 1878	Reichl, Anna	26 Jun 1875	66		27 Oct 1914	IL	B
8 May 1878	Reichl, John	27 Feb 1868	66		1 Jul 1927	IL	B
8 May 1878	Reichl, Maria	7 Sep 1870	66		26 Nov 1913	IL	B
8 May 1878	Reichl, Theresia	23 Oct 1862	66		5 Dec 1914		B
8 May 1878	Reichl, Wenceslaus	31 Aug 1865	66		1931	IL	B
8 May 1878	Reichl, Wenzl	3 Oct 1821	66	Katharina Bauer	15 Jul 1879	IL	B
4 Apr 1884	Reichl, Barbara	12 Nov 1826	66	Joseph Steiner	30 Aug 1917		B
4 Apr 1884	Steiner, Barbara	17 Oct 1859	51	John Leibl	24 Aug 1932		B
Jul 1896	Bachmann, Joseph Anton	19 Aug 1881			16 Jun 1949	WI-M	B
16 May 1901	Bachmann, Ferdinand	13 Jun 1886			17 Feb 1955	WI-M	B
PARISH - Neudorf / Trstěnice							
Neudorf / Trstěnice							
4 Nov 1856	Heimerl, Elizabeth	21 Oct 1847	20				B
4 Nov 1856	Heimerl, Eva	27 Jul 1845	20	Lorenz Kobriger	15 May 1896	WI-C	B
4 Nov 1856	Heimerl, John	6 Jan 1853	20	Anna Magdalena Meier	10 Jan 1919	WI-C	B
4 Nov 1856	Heimerl, Joseph	15 Jun 1814		Catherine Ries	15 Oct 1891	WI-C	MARR
PARISH - Ober Kozolup / Horní Kozolupy							
Mariafels / Slavice							

Abt 1868	Traegner, Anna	4 Dec 1845	44		23 May 1924	MN-N	B
Abt 1869	Grosam, George	15 Jul 1840	21	Katharina Traegner	1897	MN-N	B
Abt 1871	Grosam, Johann	5 Oct 1842	21	Maria Traegner	1 Feb 1890	MN-N	B
Abt 1864	Traegner, Albert	20 Dec 1852	44		23 Aug 1921	MN-N	B
5 Aug 1871	Heyeis, Elisabetha	1819		Adam Traegner		MN-N	TBV
5 Aug 1871	Traegner, Katharina	24 Nov 1847	44	George Grosam	21 Aug 1923	MN-N	B
5 Aug 1871	Traegner, Maria	15 May 1850	44	Johann Grosam	12 Mar 1929	MN-N	B
5 Aug 1871	Traegner, Theresia	29 Mar 1858	44		Aft 1888	MN-RN	B
PARISH - Ober-Sekeřan v/vHorní Sekyřany							
Hernmannshütte / Heřmanova Huť							
Bef 1955	Kubicek, Franz	6 Sep 1879		Aloysia Helgert	5 Sep 1955	WI-M	B
UnterSekerchan / Dolní Sekyřany							
Bef 1939	Tischler, Anna	8 Jan 1862		Anton Patz	16 Mar 1939	OH	B
PARISH - Ottenreuth / Otín							
Goldwag / Řešanov							
1 Jun 1874	Gebhart, Martin	24 Sep 1858	19	Catherine Kern	3 Jun 1943	WI-C	B
12 Jun 1875	Lerch, Katharina	20 Oct 1858	17	Franz Joseph Reinl	11 Dec 1886	WI-C	B
12 Jun 1875	Lerch, Martin	29 Sep 1824	11	Anna Seidler	4 Sep 1904	ND	B
12 Jun 1875	Lerch, Mary	15 Aug 1860	17		5 Aug 1946	ND	B
12 Jun 1875	Lerch, Michael	24 Sep 1854	19	Mary Reinl	1936	WI-C	B
12 Jun 1875	*Lerch, Michael	24 Sep 1854	19	Elizabeth Suttner	1936	WI-C	B
12 Jun 1875	Lerch, Theresa	8 Jul 1866	17		5 Mar 1933	ND	B
12 Jun 1875	Seidler, Andreas	12 Jun 1850	19		30 Mar 1901	WI-W	B
12 Jun 1875	Seidler, Anna	28 Oct 1825		Martin Lerch	3 Apr 1910	ND	TBV

12 Jun 1875	*Seidler, Anna	28 Oct 1825			3 Apr 1910	ND	TBV
Gröna / Krinov							
Abt 1869	Gebhart, Adam	13 Jul 1833	14	Maria Thurmer	16 Feb 1918	WI-C	B
Kiesenreuth / Křiženec							
18 Jun 1868	Suttner, Andreas	30 Oct 1854		Elizabeth Keuler	22 Jan 1937	WI-C	TBV
18 Jun 1868	Suttner, Anton	13 Jun 1858			Bef 1938		TBV
18 Jun 1868	Suttner, Johann	24 Apr 1815	02	Margaret Gebhart	9 Apr 1897	WI-C	B
18 Jun 1868	Suttner, Wenzel	24 Nov 1860		Bertha Nisler	23 Oct 1938	WI-C	TBV
2 Jul 1896	Suttner, Anna Maria	11 Sep 1869	02	Louis Maier	23 Nov 1961	WI-C	TBV
2 Jul 1896	Suttner, Katharina	26 Nov 1817	02	Josef Hoerl	23 Aug 1901	WI-C	B
PARISH - Pfraumberg / Přimda							
Pfraumberg / Přimda							
6 Aug 1852	Roppert, Magdelene	1808		Anton Schwind			MARR
6 Aug 1852	Schwind, Anton	18 Aug 1841	103				B
6 Aug 1852	Schwind, Bartel	8 Aug 1837	141				B
6 Aug 1852	Schwind, Dorothea	5 Feb 1836	141				B
6 Aug 1852	Schwind, Julianna	20 Dec 1845	041				B
6 Aug 1852	Schwind, Anton	21 Apr 1810	042	Magdelene Roppert			B
PARISH - Pilsen / Plzeň							
Pilsen / Plzeň							
17 Aug 1854	Cech, Vincenz	26 Sep 1823	213	Anna Utschig			B

PARISH - Prostibor / Prostiboř							
Mezholec / Mezholezy							
30 Dec 1874	Lodes, Anna	14 May 1839	23	Unknown Unknown	30 Jan 1903	WI-C	B
30 Dec 1874	*Lodes, Anna	14 May 1839	23	Wendelin Miller	30 Jan 1903	WI-C	B
Tinchau / Tuněchody							
1 Apr 1871	Wilhelm, Maria	4 Jun 1825	03	Anton Sprenger	5 Aug 1893		B
Zapfenmühle / Zapfen Mill							
16 Jun 1870	Lodes, Anton	12 Jun 1841	38	Anna Maria Neubauer	30 Nov 1893	WI-C	B
12 Jun 1873	Lodes, Wenzel	10 Dec 1843	38	Anna Steiner	19 Feb 1916	IA-PA	B
PARISH - Punnau / Boněnov							
Deutsch Thomaschlag / Domaslavičky							
6 Aug 1856	Heimrath, Marianna	2 Oct 1811	07	Jacob Franz Schmidt			B
6 Aug 1856	Schmidt, Jacob Franz	25 Jul 1800	11	Marianna Heimrath	8 Apr 1869		B
18 Jun 1868	Mayer, Theresia	11 Feb 1836	16	Michael Schicker	9 Oct 1899	WI-C	B
23 May 1870	Heimrath, Katherine	22 Aug 1819	07	Joseph Koehler	1 Jun 1898	WI-C	B
PARISH - Sankt Adalbert / Svatý Vojtěch							
Deutsch Borau / Beranovka							
18 Jun 1868	Koehler, Wenzel	9 May 1850	19	Theresa Gubka	11 Feb 1931	WI-C	B
18 Jun 1868	Schicker, Anna	1863			1946	WI-O	TBV
18 Jun 1868	Schicker, Margretha	16 Sep 1865	21		1904	WI-C	B

18 Jun 1868	Schicker, Michael	19 May 1867	21		14 Mar 1933	WI-M	B
18 Jun 1868	Suttner, Elizabeth	16 Dec 1862	03	Michael Lerch	1938	WI-C	B
4 Jun 1869	Koehler, Franz Joseph	10 Aug 1836	19	Theresia Koehler	29 Aug 1910	WI-FDL	B
4 Jun 1869	Koehler, Theresia	9 Jan 1841	19	Franz Joseph Koehler	24 Feb 1913	WI-FDL	B
23 May 1870	Koehler, Elizabeth	14 Dec 1855	19	John Ott	15 Feb 1924	WI-C	B
23 May 1870	Koehler, Franz Joseph	23 May 1859	19		28 Sep 1940	WI-C	B
23 May 1870	Koehler, Joseph	7 Oct 1818	19	Katherine Heimrath	4 Apr 1908	WI-C	B
20 Nov 1871	Scherbaum, Theresa	25 Nov 1833		Wenzel Koehler	1928	KS	TBV
20 Nov 1871	Koehler, Anna	1862			Aft 1920		TBV
20 Nov 1871	Koehler, Charles	1864			10 Sep 1931	KS	TBV
20 Nov 1871	Koehler, Theresa	15 Feb 1865			8 Jun 1947	KS	TBV
20 Nov 1871	Koehler, Wenzel	13 Mar 1834	19	Theresa Scherbaum	16 Sep 1921	KS	B
Bef 1880	Koehler, Frank	7 Jan 1815	19				B
Oct 1911	Hammer, Michael	3 Aug 1872	04	Albina Kogerer	28 Aug 1948	WI-C	B
Sankt Adalbert / Svatý Vojtěch							
7 Aug 1867	Buchtinger, Theresia	9 Apr 1836		Andreas Nadler	12 May 1909	WI-C	B
18 Jun 1868	Taubel, Anna	18 Jan 1866	13		11 Feb 1890	WI-C	B
PARISH - Schönwald / Lesná							
Schönwald / Lesná							
22 May 1873	Letz, John Adam	26 Feb 1840	21	Anna Zeidler	9 May 1915	WI-M	B
14 Jun 1880	Radl, Catherine	25 Nov 1853	09	Frank Steiner	17 Jan 1930	MN-RA	B
14 Jun 1880	Steiner, Frank	6 Mar 1853	19	Catherine Radl	18 Sep 1943	MN-RA	B
14 Jun 1880	Steiner, George	30 Nov 1878	57		13 Mar 1948	MN-RA	B
4 Apr 1884	Steiner, John	12 Oct 1850	20		4 Apr 1904		B
4 Apr 1884	Steiner, Josef	2 Dec 1866	01		20 Nov 1931		B

PARISH - Tachau / Tachov							
Ulliersreith / Oldřichov							
20 Dec 1880	Frotschl, Charles	Mar 1874					TBV
20 Dec 1880	Frotschl, Georg	1865					TBV
20 Dec 1880	Frotschl, Johann	9 Jul 1839	17	Marie Knoll	9 Jan 1908		B
20 Dec 1880	Frotschl, Johann	1862					TBV
20 Dec 1880	Frotschl, Marie	1871					TBV
20 Dec 1880	Knoll, Marie	1841		Johann Frotschl			TBV
PARISH - Tepl Stift / Teplá-klášter							
Pöken / Pěkovice							
18 Jun 1868	Braun, Elizabeth	9 Sep 1833	24	Wenzel Taubel	29 Jul 1912	WI-C	B
18 Jun 1868	Taubel, Catherine	20 Aug 1829	20				B
18 Jun 1868	Taubel, Wenzel	1 Sep 1834	20	Elizabeth Braun	19 Aug 1909	WI-C	B
PARISH - Theusing / Toužim							
Sattl / Sedlo							
1 Sep 1855	Wettstein, Adrian	29 Aug 1846	21	Catherine Mauer	4 Aug 1923	WI-FDL	B
1 Sep 1855	Wettstein, Anna	1 Nov 1839	21	Hubert Guelig	5 Sep 1872	WI-FDL	B
1 Sep 1855	Wettstein, Carl	28 Feb 1844	21	Anna Kutzer	20 May 1922	WI-C	B
1 Sep 1855	Wettstein, Edward	22 Sep 1854	21	Louise Lenz	3 Jul 1917	SD	B
1 Sep 1855	Wettstein, Frank	20 Jan 1837	21	Elizabeth Leitner	21 May 1905	WI-C	B
1 Sep 1855	Wettstein, Joseph	16 Nov 1810	21	Frances Fuhr	23 Dec 1886	WI-C	B
1 Sep 1855	Wettstein, Joseph	13 Feb 1842	21	Katherine Hoffmann	8 Mar 1895	WI-C	B
1 Sep 1855	Wettstein, Stephan	25 Feb 1850	21	Anna Maria Mauer	9 Feb 1923	WI-C	B

PARISH - Trinkseifen / Rudné							
Hochofen / Vysoká Pec							
3 Jul 1854	Noworatzky, Franz	2 Nov 1799		Anna Johanna Gevia Elster	19 Sep 1874	WI-Mw	TBV
6 Dec 1858	Elster, Anna Johanna Gevia	23 Jan 1817		Bernhard Schnurr	30 Jul 1880	WI-Mw	TBV
6 Dec 1858	*Elster, Anna Johanna Gevia	23 Jan 1817		Franz Noworatzky	30 Jul 1880	WI-Mw	TBV
6 Dec 1858	Noworatzky, Frank	15 Mar 1851	78		25 Oct 1930	WI-O	B
6 Dec 1858	Noworatzky, Joseph	2 Sep 1854	78		23 Nov 1941	WI-Mw	B
6 Dec 1858	Schneier, Adolph	24 Sep 1858	78		1859	WI-Mw	B
6 Dec 1858	Schnurr, Anton	26 Jul 1841			8 Feb 1913	WI-Mw	TBV
6 Dec 1858	Schnurr, Magdalena	22 Jul 1838			9 Mar 1920	WI-Mw	TBV
PARISH - Tschernoschin / Černošín							
Wolfersdorf / Olbramov							
1 Jun 1874	Seidler, Katharina	19 Feb 1835	40	Wenzel Gebhart	9 Oct 1919	ND	B
Abt 1889	Rosch, Anna	30 Apr 1855	12	Wendelin Pimpl	18 Apr 1946	MN-S	B
PARISH - Tutz / Dubec							
Pössigkau / Bezděkov							
Abt 1865	Martinka, George	10 Jan 1850	38	Barbara L Kachelmeier	1930	MN-B	B
Apr 1868	Zishka, Barbara	Jan 1816		George Martinka	1902	MN-B	MARR
Abt 1869	Martinka, Barbara	5 Oct 1844	45	John Schottenbauer	Dec 1876	MN-N	B
Abt 1869	Schatenbauer, George	3 Aug 1865	46		22 Feb 1954	MN-RW	B
Abt 1869	Schottenbauer, John	18 Jan 1838	05	Barbara Martinka	1 Jan 1918	MN-RW	B
Abt 1869	*Schottenbauer, John	18 Jan 1838	05	Anna Hegert	1 Jan 1918	MN-RW	B
22 May 1880	Martinka, Wenzel	5 May 1853	45				B
May 1893	Wild, Mary	19 Feb 1845	39	Joseph Lang	4 Dec 1909		B

Zemschen / Třemešné							
11 May 1868	Buchl, Elizabeth	9 Oct 1837	27	Johann Goblirsch	26 Apr 1909	MN-N	B
11 May 1868	Goblirsch, Adam	15 Jan 1862	05		11 Apr 1946	MN-N	B
11 May 1868	Goblirsch, Adam	6 Jul 1839	05	Margaretha Stadick	19 Sep 1908	MN-N	B
11 May 1868	Goblirsch, George	9 May 1867	24		Bef 1880		B
11 May 1868	Goblirsch, Johann	18 Sep 1835	05	Elizabeth Buchl	26 Feb 1909	MN-N	B
11 May 1868	Goblirsch, John	20 Oct 1867	05	Anne Muehlbauer	7 Jul 1941	MN-RW	B
11 May 1868	Goblirsch, Mary	22 Sep 1865	38		27 Jan 1937		B
11 May 1868	Golblirsch, George Anton	9 Jan 1865	05	Mary Goblirsch	3 Apr 1922	MN-RW	B
11 May 1868	Stadick, Margaretha	23 May 1841	38	Adam Goblirsch	15 Jan 1917	MN-N	B
4 Jun 1869	Goblirsch, Joseph John	11 Mar 1831	10	Katherine Marie Schloegl	1 Apr 1913	MN-B	B
4 Jun 1869	Schloegl, Katherine Marie	9 Nov 1837	25	Joseph John Goblirsch	23 Feb 1932	MN-B	B
PARISH - Unter Jamny / Dolni Jamné							
Schwitz / Svetec							
14 Jul 1868	Gubka, Joseph Michael	19 Jan 1833	07	Mary Anna Theresa Turba	12 Mar 1925	SD	B
PARISH - Welperschitz / Erpužice							
Lomitschka / Lomnička							
9 Aug 1873	Hammer, Engelbert	7 Apr 1872			19 Aug 1958	WI-FDL	TBV
9 Aug 1873	Hammer, Joseph	1869			21 Jan 1931	WI-FDL	TBV
9 Aug 1873	Hammer, Mathias	1837		Katharina Theyerl	11 May 1898	WI-FDL	TBV
9 Aug 1873	Schroedl, Kordula	10 Dec 1814	04	Gregor Theyerl	19 Mar 1878		B
9 Aug 1873	Theyerl, Gregor	15 Oct 1816	06	Kordula Schroedl	8 Feb 1903		B
9 Aug 1873	Theyerl, Joseph	20 Feb 1838	06		24 Oct 1914	WI-FDL	B
9 Aug 1873	Theyerl, Katharina	19 Jul 1844	06	Mathias Hammer	10 Mar 1918	WI-FDL	B

9 Aug 1873	Theyerl, Lorenz	28 Oct 1846			17 Apr 1923	WI-C	TBV
Bef 1880	Theyerl, Anton	31 May 1836	04	Anna Saazer	30 May 1895		B
PARISH - Witschin / Vidžín							
Dobrawod / Dobrá Voda							
Jun 1869	Holtschick, Maria Anna	18 May 1834	01	Joseph Zepnick	7 Sep 1870	WI-C	B
Jun 1869	*Holtschick, Maria Anna	18 May 1834	01		7 Sep 1870	WI-C	B
Neschikau / Nežichov							
18 Jun 1868	Heidl, Theresia	20 Oct 1814	01	Anton Schicker	21 Jun 1900	WI-C	B
18 Jun 1868	Schicker, Michael	15 Dec 1836	01	Theresia Mayer	21 Jan 1921	WI-C	B
15 Jun 1910	*Schicker, Michael	15 Dec 1836	01	Theresia Mayer	21 Jan 1921	WI-C	B
Special Designations:				**Months:**			
Abt = About				01 = Jan = January			
Aft = After				02 = Feb = February			
Bef = Before				03 = Mar = March			
				04 = Apr = April			
*Name = Multiple marriages				05 = May = May			
**Name = Multiple trips to the United States				06 = Jun = June			
				07 = Jul = July			
Record Types:				08 = Aug = August			
B = Baptismal and/or Christening Record				09 = Sep = September			
MARR = Marriage Record				10 = Oct = October			
TBV = To Be Verified				11 = Nov = November			
				12 = Dec = December			

Chapter 5

Conclusion

This is the story of hundreds of German Bohemians who emigrated from the Tepl and Marienbad areas of today's Czech Republic beginning in the 1850s. They traveled by sea and land to Calumet County, Wisconsin. They bought land, cleared forests for farmland and built log cabins. They are among the early settlers of Calumet County.

The Immigration Research Study pinpointed the origins of 248 Town of Brothertown German Bohemians. Other German Bohemians who settled in surrounding areas also were identified.

We know their names. In many cases, we know their ancestors' names. Resources are available to provide German Bohemian village histories with the social, economic, and political context in which they lived.

Perhaps one question is left to answer: Why did German Bohemians settle in Calumet County? For the answer we turn again to the Calumet County community. An 1867 article from *The Chilton Times* gives reasons for the wave of German Bohemian immigration:

The Chilton Times
April 27, 1867, Front Page

> The season of emigration is now fairly open and thousands have already arrived from the old country in the United States and thousands are now on their way. Nearly all of them will come West to find a home. Quite a number has arrived in New Holstein in this county. We therefore wish to speak of a few advantages to be derived by emigrants and others by settling in the County of Calumet, as we believe there is no county in Wisconsin that can offer greater inducements to emigrants than

ours, and there will never be a better time to buy the foundation of a good farm at a low price, than the present season. Every part of the county is now opened by roads leading to good markets, and the farmer can take his produce to Fond du Lac, Manitowoc, Sheboygan, Island City, Appleton or Green Bay just as he chooses. In fact there is no county in the State which has so many markets close around it.

Our land is all of a deep, vegetable mold which will make the most desirable and productive farms. No better water can be found in the State – our clear, sparkling streams which come to the surface, have long been the admiration of the traveler. We have no prairies, but we have as splendid hard wood forests, consisting of every variety of Oak, Maple, Elm, Butternut, Cherry, and Basswood, as the sun looks down upon in his day's journey, and owing to the numerous mills and manufactories which surround us, almost every tree is valuable. Our population is over ten thousand and a more prosperous, thrifty, and contented class of farmers cannot be found in the West.

In a few years, at the farthest, a rail road will be running directly through the county from Milwaukee to the Fox

> River, and we confidently believe that the Manitowoc and Menasha Railroad, which runs through some of our Northern towns will be completed in a short time, affording additional facilities to our farmers to carry their produce to market. We therefore advise all who wish to get a profitable and comfortable home to come and see the most fertile county in Wisconsin.[1]

For Calumet County residents in 1867, the value of their community was personal. They had settled in the area. Their experiences and observations offer personal insights into the reasons German Bohemians settled in Calumet County.

The developing community knew firsthand the characteristics needed for success on this virgin land: hard work, persistence, and faith in God. Our concluding words about the German Bohemian wave of immigration and its effects on Calumet County are best expressed in the words of Calumet County residents as stated in an 1869 article in *The Chilton Times*:

[1] *"Emigrants," The Chilton Times (Chilton, Wisconsin), 27 April 1867, front page. [transcribed by Joan Naomi Steiner, PhD]*

"Taken together they [German Bohemians] are the most enterprising religious congregation in the county and their zeal in the faith they profess should be imitated in every community and by every denomination."[2]

---

[2] "The St. Charles Catholic Congregation," *The Chilton Times* (Chilton, Wisconsin), 25 July 1868, front page. *[transcribed by Joan Naomi Steiner, PhD]*

Taken together, [illegible]

the [illegible]

the [illegible]

should be [illegible]

[illegible]

The [illegible] July 1936, front page [illegible]

European Hands on the Table in Wischkowitz/Výškovice (Photo courtesy of Klára Salzmann. "Renewal of Czech-German Border Landscape." Prague: Astron Studio, 2015)

Part II
Resources

Chapter 6

Local Family Histories and Area Histories

Bellin, Loretta M., and Terri L. Bellin. *The Family of Joseph Scholz & Theresia Winkler 1800-1988*. Privately printed. 1988

Descendants of the following German Bohemian families include: the **Rahmer** and **Schierl** families whose ancestors originated from **Royau**; the Groeschel [Groeschl] family whose ancestors originated from **Einseidl**; the **Reinl** family whose ancestors originated from **Abaschin**; and the **Steiner** family whose ancestors originated from **Wischezahn**.

The book is 202 pages.

Bittner, Bernadette N. and Clarence W. *Heiman Family History 1853-1987*. Privately printed. 1986.

Descendants of the **Groeschel [Groeschl]** family whose ancestors originated from Einseidl are discussed in this family history as they relate to the Heiman family. The book includes a head-of-household index.

The book is 144 pages.

Bittner, Bernadette M., and Ottila S. Wettstein. *Leitner-Nadler-Reinl Relatives Bohemia to Wisconsin 1855*. Privately printed, 1979.

The first families to emigrate from Bohemia to Calumet County, Wisconsin, are featured in this family history. Individual chapters are dedicated to the following families: **Engelbart Leitner**, **Frank Nadler**, **Anton Reinl** and **Joseph Fischer**. Miscellaneous information is found on the **Lodes** and **Anton Kocher** families. A head-of-family index is included.

The book is 178 pages.

Bittner, Bernadette M., and Ottila S. Wettstein. *The Schwobe Story,* Privately printed, unknown date.

The **Schwobe**, **Neuber** and **Heckel** families are featured in this family history. The German Bohemian families of **Egerer**, **Leitner**, **Steiner** and **Wettstein** are included.

The book is 214 pages.

Bittner, Bernadette M. *Bodendein/Kutzer Family*. Privately printed, unknown date.

The **Kutzer**, **Egerer** and **Lenz** families from **Royau** are discussed in this family history. Miscellaneous Kutzer land information is included.

The booklet is 25 pages with 10 loose pages.

Gruber, Elta. *From the main tree, we fly into the future: Daun Family Genealogy*, Privately printed, unknown date.

The descendants of Christopher **Daun** (1803-1888) whose son, John Daun (1841-1909) married **Adalbert Steiner**'s daughter Theresa (1848-1918), are detailed. Obituaries, photographs, and a list of references are included.

The book is 174 pages.

Kern, John. *A History of the Parish of St. Charles Borromeo from its beginning to 1866 to the Days of its Diamond Jubilee November 4, 1941*. Privately printed, 1941.

The Parish of St. Charles Borromeo is in Charlesburg, Town of Brothertown, Calumet County, Wisconsin. The history of the parish is the work, in large part, of the German Bohemians who emigrated from the Tepl and Marienbad areas in the early to mid-1850s. Historical beginnings of the village in 1855 along with the founding of the first church in 1866 are discussed. Founding families identified include **Lodes**, **Nadler**, **Fischer**, **Reinl**, **Lenz**, **Leitner**, **Steiner**, **Kutzer**, **Wettstein** and **Groeschel**.

The book is 89 pages.

Nolan, Leta Anne, editor. *History of Spink County Area: In Celebration of South Dakota's Centennial 1889–1989*. Dallas: Curtis Media Corporation, 1989.

The centennial book features topical histories of Spink County area cities, towns, villages, churches, organizations, societies, businesses, and townships. Short biographies and photographs tell the stories of early settlers. Of special interest is the **Lenz** family, who migrated in 1882 from Calumet and Fond du Lac counties in Wisconsin.

The book is 481 pages.

Steil, Russell; Rosalinda Schuller; Jean Reinders; Arnoldt Heldt; and Kay Perry. *Mallard, Iowa 100 Years 1882 – 1982*. Privately printed, 1982.

The centennial book features histories of area businesses, churches and community organizations. Early Wisconsin settlers who moved to Iowa are **Lodes** and **Steiner** families. Short biographies of individuals and families often include photographs.

The book is 299 pages.

Steiner, Marianne. *The Descendants of Adalbert Steiner and Anna Guentner* [Gintner] *1815-1986*. Privately printed. 1986.

The family history is organized around the descendants of **Adalbert** and **Anna Gintner Steiner's** four children: **Anton, Theresia, Franz Joseph** and **John**. A surname index is included along with maps of Europe, Calumet County, Wisconsin, and southern Minnesota.

The book is 499 pages.

Wenig, John, and Jeffrey J. Lisowe. *The Rott Family History*, Privately printed. 1978.

This is the story of **Rott** and **Koegerer** families who emigrated from **Habakladrau** and settled first in Town of Russell in Sheboygan County and later in the Town of Brothertown. The **Kuehnl** family from **Falknau** is also discussed.

The booklet is 9 pages.

Wettstein, Ottila. *Applebecker-Boll Families.* Privately printed, 1989.

Franziska **Gintner Mueller** from **Wischkowitcz** became George Applebecker's second wife in 1870. Children of this marriage are detailed.

The book is 40 pages.

Wettstein, Ottila Meyer. *Autobiography Ottila (Tillie) Meyer-Wettstein Siblings and Family.* Privately printed, May 1997.

Ottila Wettstein writes about her life and the lives of her family members. She includes photographs, family stories and reflections on her life. She also identifies families in her childhood neighborhood.

The book is approximately 30 pages.

Wettstein, Ottila Meyer. *Mueller-Koehler Families.* Privately printed, 1986.

Ottila Wettstein writes about her grandparents: Sigismund **Mueller** (1854-1933) and Anna **Koehler** (1854-1928). The history details the Mueller descendants and includes obituaries, maps, photographs and newspaper clippings. The George **Apfelbacher** family is included as a supplement.

The book is 105 pages.

Wettstein, Ottila Meyer. Wettstein's *Austria to America 1855,* Volumes I and II. Privately printed, 1988 and reprinted in 1990 and 1992.

The two-volume family history details the family of **Joseph Wettstein** and **Franziska Fuhrman** and their descendants. Newspaper articles, photographs, and an extensive index make this book highly informative. Information is included on the German Bohemian families of **Groeschel**, **Leitner**, **Mueller**, **Nadler**, **Reinl** and **Steiner**.

Volumes I and II are each 291 pages.

Woelfel, James A. *The Ulrich Woelfel Family History 1845-1995*. Privately printed. 1995.

Descendants of the **Schierl** family whose ancestors originated from **Royau** and the **Steiner** family whose ancestors originated from **Wischezahn** are found in the "Family Index with Relationships" at the end of the book. News articles, photos, and copies of original documents are also included in the family history.

The book is 307 pages.

Chapter 7

Video Documentaries of Habakladrau and Pistau Parishies, Kladruby Chapel, and United States Embassy American Center Exhibition in Prague

Habakladrau Church Festival, August 11, 2019. Privately held by Joan Naomi Steiner, PhD [ADDRESS FOR PRIVATE USE] Neenah, Wisconsin, 2019.

> The St. Lawrence Church Festival in Habakladrau is an annual village-wide event with vendors for food, handmade items, cultural dances and children's games. At 3 p.m. mass is held in the historic parish church. Churchgoers enjoy homemade sweets that are handed out at the door after mass.

Families who emigrated from Habakladrau beginning in 1855 include **Degl, Hammer, Hanika, Kogerer, Lodes, Neubauer, Pop, Rosner, Rott, Rummer, Schneider, Schusser, Steidl** and **Turba**.

Families who emigrated from Abaschin beginning in 1855 include **Denk** and **Reinl**.

The **Schusser** family emigrated from Hohendorf in 1882.

Families who emigrated from Müllestau beginning in 1855 are **Huttl**, **Windirsch** and **Wurtinger**.

Families who emigrated from Wischezahn beginning in 1856 are **Arbes**, **Lodes, Schmidt, Steiner** and **Zepnick**.

The **Gintner, Nadler** and **Zepnick** families emigrated from Wischkowitz in 1856.

Pistau Church Festival, August 26, 2019. Privately held by Joan Naomi Steiner, [ADDRESS FOR PRIVATE USE] Neenah, Wisconsin, 2019.

The St. Bartholomew Church Festival in Pistau is a 3 p.m. mass officiated by Abbot Filip Lobcowzicz of Tepl Monastery with three visiting priests from Germany. The mass is conducted in German and Czech languages. People who attend are today's Czech residents and visiting expelled Germans with their descendants. All are invited after mass for coffee and cakes in the rectory hosted by the Dr. Spata family of Pistau.

Families who emigrated from Martanau beginning in 1856 are **Hiederer** and **Pfroger**.

Families who emigrated from Wilkowitz beginning in 1855 are **Schicker**, **Schmidt**, **Schmiedl** and **Schott**.

Kladruby Chapel Dedication, August 15, 2019. Privately held by Joan Naomi Steiner, [ADDRESS FOR PRIVATE USE] Neenah, Wisconsin, 2019.

Abbot Filip Lobcowzicz of Tepl Monastery conducts a dedication service for the recently restored Kladruby Chapel. The Kladruby Chapel is located near the monastery. Many community members attended the outdoor service.

United States Embassy American Center, Prague, Czech Republic, August 16, 2022. Privately held by Joan Naomi Steiner, [ADDRESS FOR PRIVATE USE] Neenah, Wisconsin, 2022.

The 2022 Exhibition entitled "Identity Transfer across Generations" showcases five Calumet County, Wisconsin, German Bohemian families (**Lenz, Lodes, Müeller. Steiner** and **Wettstein**). The stories of these families, who moved from Western Bohemia to the U.S. in the 19th century, are told by their descendants. The exhibition also explores how today's descendants identify: as Americans? Czechs? Czech-Americans?

The opening of the exhibition features U.S. Embassy Deputy Cultural Attaché, Todd Jurkowski, U.S. Embassy American Center Director, Vít Nejedlo, and attendees from Germany, the Czech Republic and the United States. The 2022 Exhibition is the third exhibit (previously 2020 and 2021) on the topic of German Bohemian immigration to Calumet County, Wisconsin, held at the U.S. Embassy American Center. The exhibition flyer and description can be found at https://www.americkecentrum.cz/en/udalost/identity-transfer-across-generations/.

Chapter 8

Translated Books

Bartoš, Jaromir. *Surroundings of Mariánské Lázně in Vintage Postcards*. Hostivice: Baron. 2013.

Villages of Marienbad Region, especially those destroyed by World War II and Soviet control of the region, are showcased with vintage postcards collected by the Voluntary Association of Municipalities of the Microregion Mariánskolázensko. Each postcard scene is described in historical terms. The 216-page book is written in German, Czech, Russian and English.

Villages of families who emigrated are **Abaschen**, **Einsiedl**, **Habakladrau**, **Hohendorf**, **Martinau**, **Müllestau**, **Pistau**, **Rauschenbach**, **Wilkowitz** and **Wischezahn**.

Bartoš. Jaromir. *Town History in Pictures*. Blansko: Novatisk, 2018.

The history of Marienbad beginning in 1528 is detailed through photographs that are described in Czech, German, English and Russian languages. The book is 143 pages.

Families who emigrated from Marienbad beginning in 1853 include **Cech, Popp** and **Utschig**.

Salzmann, Klára. *Renewal of Czech-German Border Landscape*. Prague: Astron Studio, 2015.

The book explores the landscape revival of today's Czech Republic border, which was destroyed by the events of World War II and Soviet control of the region. In the village of **Wischkowitz,** home of the **Gintner, Nadler** and **Zepnick** families who emigrated beginning in 1856, an international workshop was held in 2014 to discuss what should happen to the border areas and villages like **Wischkowitz**.

The project was supported by the Cross-border Cooperation Programme Objective 3 Czech Republic-Free State of Bavaria. The 201-page book is written in German, Czech and English.

Chapter 9

Czech Resources: Local Historians, Local Museums and Books

Local historians and museums as well as books written in Czech are available for learning about our German Bohemian ancestors who once lived in the villages of the Marienbad and Tepl areas. I briefly share my research experiences in hopes they will offer other researchers some possibilities on how to approach learning about German Bohemian ancestors who once lived in today's Czech Republic.

Local Historians

My story begins with a meeting with the mayor of my parish village Habakladrau before my first onsite visit. I also arranged for a translator to accompany me to the area. Mayor Aurelie Skřivanová escorted us on an informative tour of the church, school, rectory, cemetery and parish. Mayor Skřivanová also gave me a book authored by two local historians about Habakladrau, Wischezahn, and Wischkowitz.[1] My direct ancestral lines are traced to all three villages.

I returned in 2018 for a second visit to Habakladrau. Mayor Skřivanová arranged a meeting with Zdeněk Buchtele, one of the authors of the book she had given me the year before. I had prepared interview questions about the villages and parish and with a translator conducted the interview. Buchtele invited me to visit his local history museum in Manský Dvůr. He also invited his associate Jana Drahokoupilová, who worked for the local Marienbad newspaper. We toured Buchtele's local history museum. I learned about daily life in my homeland villages and how changing political situations have affected the area.

---

[1] Zdeněk Buchtele, and Richard Švandrlik. *Ovesné Kladruby a zaniklé obce Vysočany a Výškovice.* (Planá u Mariánských Lázni: Nakladatelstelství a vydavatelstvío Knourek, 2012).

Drahokoupilová interviewed me over lunch in a local pub. Her news article combined both my museum visit and the interview.[2]

Strana 3 MARIÁNSKOLÁZEŇSKÉ NOVINY 22. červen 2018

ZPRÁVY Z MARIÁNSKÝCH LÁZNÍ

Jak se hledají kořeny rodu. Joan Naomi Steiner je našla nedaleko Mariánských Lázní

Náhoda tomu chtěla, že Zdeněk Buchtele pozval redakci na setkání s americkou dámou Joan Naomi Maltby Steiner, která v našem regionu hledá kořeny svého rodu. A protože hledá důkladně, chtěla poznat i minimuzeum jmenovaného vlastivědníka na Manském dvoře, aby se lépe orientovala v životě Čechů. Proto se naše setkání uskutečnilo právě tam.

Při zpáteční cestě a zastávce v Dolním Žandově jsem Joan, příjemnou, kontaktní a velmi vitální dámu, která kraj projíždí s tlumočnicí, trochu vyzpovidala. - **Amerika je na hledání předků v Čechách trochu z ruky, jak to děláte?** – „Musím Vám říct, že jsme všichni mysleli, že naši praprapraředkové žili v Německu (nakonec i jméno tomu odpovídalo), teprve nedávno jsem se dozvěděla, že vlastně pocházíme z Čech, a to mě teprve začalo zajímat. Obrátila jsem se přes internet na společnost, která nese název Česko – německá společnost národního dědictví v USA a loni jsem tu právě s touto společností byla poprvé. Už jsem věděla, že asi pocházíme z okolí Ovesných Kladrub a setkala jsem se s paní starostkou Aurélií Skřivanovou a také s knihou o této obci. Moji předkové pocházejí z obce Vysočany, Adalbert Steiner odešel do Ameriky v roce 1856. (Vysočany zmizely jako mnoho obcí v regionu, zbyl pouze jeden téměř rozpadlý statek, shodou okolností právě ten, který patřil Adalbertu Steinerovi, nicméně dnes je prý už téměř opravený). Není bez zajímavosti, že ti, kteří odešli, v Americe postavili úplně novou vesnici „na zelené louce", lépe řečeno doslova urvali pozemky lesům. Druhá větev Steinerů zůstala v Čechách a paní Joan, která je čtvrtou generací žijící v Americe, našla v Ovesných Kladrubech hrob svého předka Franze Josepha Steinera. Podle jejích slov je nadšená, že Steinerové pocházejí právě odsud, moc se jí tu líbí nejen krajina, ale také vstřícní lidé. Své poznatky i fotografický materiál bude dál pečlivě zpracovávat. Byla jsem moc ráda, že jsem potkala člověka, který pro objasnění svých kořenů je ochoten projet tisíce kilometrů, obětovat nejen čas, ale samozřejmě i nemalé peníze. Těší mě, že ty kořeny našla Joan právě u nás a že jí k tomu všichni ochotně pomohli. *(Jana Drahokoupilová)*

Joan Steinerová (uprostřed) se o všechno živě zajímala. Zleva Zdeněk Buchtele, Joan Steinerová a tlumočnice. Foto Jana Drahokoupilová

Zastupitelstvo přiklepl o organizaci milión, který vedení města původně zamítlo

Mariánskolázeňští zastupitelé schválili zdejšímu domovu pro seniory příspěvek milión korun. Jednalo se o podporu, aby kvůli chybějícím financím nedošlo k ohrožení provozu zařízení. Na zastupitelstvu ale nezaznělo, že když o tyto prostředky organizace žádala poprvé, město jí je neschválilo.

„Je to zkrátka o tom, že se jim nedostává finančních prostředků a je to z důvodu navyšování mezd, se kterými se nepočítalo v době, kdy byl rozpočet na letošní rok schvalován," odůvodnil pirátský starosta Martin Kalina návrh usnesení.

Příspěvková organizace Domov pro seniory ale předložila vedení města návrh svého rozpočtu už v srpnu 2017, tedy čtyři měsíce před schvalováním městského rozpočtu. „Jejich návrh rozpočtu s navýšením mezd počítal, ale nedostali od města finance v požadované výši," potvrdila Yvona Švejnohová, vedoucí odboru financí. K navyšování mezd, kterým starosta na květnovém zastupitelstvu zdůvodnil finanční příspěvek, ale došlo již v červenci, respektive v listopadu 2017. Jestli se v prosinci 2017, kdy zastupitelé schvalovali rozpočet, tedy již vědělo o navyšování mezd, starosta uvedl, že „podle tisku předloženého na květnovém zastupitelstvu zjevně ne." Předkladatelem tisku byl právě lázeňský starosta a není zřejmé, kdo přesně s navýšením mezd při schvalování rozpočtu na letošní rok nepočítal, protože vedení města mělo tyto podklady k dispozici, když původní požadavek organizaci zamítlo. Jestli tyto informace neměl nynější starosta, který byl v době schvalování rozpočtu radním, pak měl tedy asi být informován svým stranicnkým předchůdcem Petrem Třešňákem. *(Jiří Škroch)*

[2] "Jak se hledají kořeny rodu. Joan Naomi Steiner je našla nedaleko Mariánských Lázní," Mariánskolázeňské Noviny (Mariánskolázeňské, Czech Republic), 22 červen 2018, ročník VI, strana 3.

Following is Marie Zahn's translation of the news article:

How to find roots of the family

Joan Naomi Steiner found them not far from Mariánské Lázně

It was by sheer luck that Zdeněk Buchtele invited our newspaper to meet the American woman, Mrs. Joan Naomi Maltby Steiner. She was looking for the roots of her family in our region. And because she was looking well, she wanted to get to know a museum of already mentioned historian in Manský Dvůr, to get more familiar with the life of Czechs. That is why our meeting took place exactly in the museum.

On our way back we stopped in Dolní Žandov and I had a chance to ask some questions to Joan, this pleasant, sociable, and very vital lady, who traveled through our region with an interpreter.

America is quite a distance for someone looking for their ancestry in Bohemia. How do you manage this?

I have to tell you first that we all were thinking that our ancestors had lived in Germany (even their names supported that). Not a long time ago I found out that in fact we originated in Bohemia and then I started to be interested. I contacted a society with the name Czech – German Society of National Heritage [German Bohemian Heritage Society] in the USA last year via the internet.

Last year I visited this area for the first time with this society. By then I already knew that my people came from the area of Ovesné Kladruby. I met the mayor, Aurélie Skřivanová, and saw a book about this village. My ances-

> tors came from the village of Vysočany. Adalbert Steiner left for America in the year 1856. (Vysočany disappeared as many villages in this region. Only one farmhouse, almost half destroyed, remained standing. Coincidentally it is the house that was owned by [a cousin of] Adalbert Steiner. Today the farmhouse is almost completely renovated.) It is interesting that those who left, built in America a very new village on a "green meadow."
>
> They took land from the forest. A second branch of the Steiner family stayed in Bohemia. Joan, who is the fourth [third] generation born in America, found a grave of her ancestor Franz Joseph Steiner in Ovesné Kladruby. According to her, she is excited that Steiners came from this area. She likes the countryside as well as the forth coming people. The collected information as well as photographs she will carefully organize. I was so happy to meet a person who was willing to travel thousands of kilometers, dedicating not only time but money as well, to learn about her ancestors. I am glad that her roots were found here and that everyone was willing to help her.[3]

Local people in the area learned about my research through the news article. People from the area were willing to meet me and to help me with the research when I returned in 2019. This warm reception is credited to Jana Drahokoupilová and her news article introducing me and my research interest in the area. Information about the museum is found at https://www.infocesko.cz/content/zapadoceske-lazne-krusne-hory-zapad-kultura-muzea-regionalni-mini-museum-mansky-dvur-dolni-zandov.aspx.

---

[3] Marie Zahn, translator, "Jak se hledají kořeny rodu. Joan Naomi Steiner je našla nedaleko Mariánských Lázní," Mariánskolázeňské Noviny (Mariánskolázeňské, Czech Republic), 22 červen 2018, ročník VI, strana 3.

In the same issue of the newspaper, Drahokoupilová has a second article, an interview with Zdeněk Buchtele.[4]

Strana 7 MARIÁNSKOLÁZEŇSKÉ NOVINY 22. červen 2018

BONUSOVÁ PŘÍLOHA - OSOBNOSTI

Zdeněk Buchtele: S Richardem Švandrlíkem jsme psali o všem, co se nám podařilo najít

Mariánskolázeňské listy a posléze noviny využívají už léta články a poznatky o historii zdejšího regionu Zdeňka Buchteleho, je na čase, aby lidé poznali také osobnost tohoto neúnavného vlastivědníka a archeologa.

Žijete ve Velké Hleďsebi od narození? Narodil jsem se v Mariánských Lázních, ale žil jsem v Drmoulu – učení, vojna, po vojně jsem bydlel v Mariánských Lázních a od roku 1980 v Hleďsebi.

Jaké je Vaše civilní povolání? Černé řemeslo (krátce jako zámečník, poté u oblastní PBH v ML jako vodoinstalatér), pak jako údržbář POTRAVINY Cheb. Po roce 1990 jako OSVČ a od r. 2010 v důchodu).

Kdy jste se začal zajímat o historii tohoto kraje, jsou v tom geny? Mamka se zajímala o historii, ale spíše o šlechtické a královské rodokmeny. Možná, že to byl základ pro moji činnost. Mě zaujal spíše praktický život nejen šlechty, ale i obyčejných lidí od pravěku, až do doby středověku. Pro značnou absenci takovýchto zpráv z tohoto období v naší oblasti jsem se začal o tyto příběhy zajímat. Aktivně asi tak po roce 1973, kdy jsem objevil několik pravěkých střepů u dvora Lískovec.

Zdeněk Buchtele. Foto Jiří Škroch

Měl jste nějaký systém v monitorování regionu? Je několik zásadních věcí: v případě zaniklého osídlení je třeba hledat místa, kde je voda, kudy vedly cesty a kde se mohlo hospodařit třeba na malých a drobných plochách. Ve starých soupisech osad a sídel byl také řád. Jednotlivá místa bývala vždy popisována v pořadí za sebou v určitém směru. Dalo se proto usuzovat, že při určité hustotě tehdejšího osídlení, bude v dalším předpokládaném místě možnost objevu další osady. Takže určitý systém mám, ale někdy je to také vyloženě o náhodě a pak se třeba dá následně i ten systém využít.

Pokud vím, všechno jste pečlivě zapisoval, měřil, zakresloval. Čeho jste si hlavně všímal? Ano, to je pravda. Někdy kresba je víc než fotografie, obzvlášť, když jsou připojeny rozměry. Udělal jsem mnoho plánků a nákresů různých objevených věcí a objektů. V případě drobných památek to často posloužilo policii, která si u mne vyzvedávala podklady ke ztraceným předmětům, aby mohla následně vyčíslit jejich cenu. Všímal jsem si hlavně věcí poškozených a zničených, kterých mi bylo vždy líto. Často jsem se pokoušel (někdy zbytečně) o jejich záchranu.

S kým jste spolupracoval? Měli jste rozdělené role? Spolupracovníků bylo střídavě více, ale jeden byl „stálý". Od roku 1974, prakticky nepřetržitě jsme spolupracovali. Byl to Ing. Richard Švandrlík. On ekonom, já praktik. On častěji po archívech, já častěji v terénu. A pak jsme psali o všem, co se nám podařilo najít, vzájemně to doplňovali a upravovali.

Ale spolupracoval jste také s Československou akademií věd? O přímou spolupráci nešlo, ale mnoho publikací vydaných ČSAV čerpalo a dodnes čerpá z mých výzkumů a k nim vydaných zpráv. Po roce 1989 se společnost přejmenovala na „Česká archeologická společnost při ČSAV", kde jsem byl asi do roku 2014.

Vydali jste s panem Švandrlíkem spoustu publikací o regionu, kolik jich bylo? S kolegou Švandrlíkem jsme společně vydali asi 25 publikací a desítky článků, zpráv a informací. Z mé samostatné činnosti uvedu asi 7 vlastních publikací a další desítky článků, hlášenek a zpráv. Vše je o historii regionu kolem Mar. Lázní.

Vím, že máte Mariánskolázeňsko důkladně zmonitorované a také vím, že jste se pokusil zachránit hrad Vildštejn, i když to tenkrát nedopadlo dobře. Nedopadlo to dobře pro naši další činnost, ale dopadlo to dobře pro vlastní hrad. Záchranné práce, které jsme těch pět let na něm prováděli, ho zachránily před zřícením, které mu tehdy podle statika hrozilo takřka ihned. Jeho zkázu jsme tak zažehnali a dneska hrad stojí, a i když je bohužel v soukromých rukou, je přístupný a slouží veřejnosti.

Který byl Váš nejzajímavější nález nebo objev? Jako nejzajímavější nález považuji žulový kámen, nalezený pod kopcem Podhora. Jeho spodní část má tvar srdce, nahoru se mění do tvaru vejce. Oba tvary od sebe odděluje tmavá žilka po celém obvodu. Srdce a vejce byly vždy považovány za symboly života. V horní části je patrný reliéf Krista ze stran obklopený „mandorlou"- jakousi dvojitou svatozáři. V takovéto úpravě můžeme vznik předmětu datovat do období kolem roku 1000. Poté se mandorla už objevuje pouze jako malba na soklech kaplí a kostelů.

Nejzajímavější nález Zdeňka Buchteleho – kultovní kámen s mandorlou. Foto Zdeněk Buchtele

Ještě pokračujete ve svých výpravách? Pokračuji, stále je co objevovat, ale trochu mě přibrzdilo kompletní předělání expozic v muzeu na Manském dvoře, kde už byly jednotlivé předměty soustředěny k sobě do určitých celků, takže expozice nepůsobí chaoticky. Další „brzdou" jsou roky, které přibývají a člověk už se nepohybuje tak čile jako dřív. Mezitím stále píšu o dalších zajímavostech, bylo by škoda, kdyby někam zapadly. V současné době je to historie obce Hamrníky.

(Jana Drahokoupilová)

Jubilant Rudolf Poláček provozoval trojkombinaci hokej, fotbal a tenis

Někdy po roce 1945, to bylo Rudolfu Poláčkovi sedmnáct let a byl po vyučení číšníkem, se rodina Poláčkových přestěhovala do Mariánských Lázní. Energií nabitý mladík se pak začátkem padesátých let vrhl naplno do sportování v místních klubech. V zimě hokej, v létě fotbal a jako doplněk ještě tenis. Tato trojkombinace nebyla v té době nijak výjimečná.

Jeho parketou byla v obou zmíněných kolektivních sportech obrana. Ve fotbalu, v němž kopal B a A třídu, proslul jako nesmlouvavý stoper a stejně tak i v hokeji coby krajní obránce v oblastních soutěžích. Až do poloviny šedesátých let to znamenalo stovky zápasů. O počtu natrénovaných hodin ani nemluvě. Pak přišla mezi roky 1966 - 70 sportovní přestávka, kdy Rudolf Poláček dlel profesně v Garmisch Partenkirchenu. Alespoň měl v roce 1967 možnost zhlédnout MS v hokeji, které se hrálo ve Vídni a kde naši skončili čtvrtí.

Po návratu do Mariánských Lázní se opět zapojil do sportovního dění. Tentokrát jako hokejový trenér. Pod jeho vedením se vytvořila vynikající parta, která v roce 1973 vyhrála impozantním způsobem krajský přebor, a to bez ztráty jediného bodu! Poláček byl tehdy vyhodnocen jako nejlepší trenér soutěže. Přišla slavná éra v divizi a posléze ve II. lize, kdy na lázeňský hokej chodily návštěvy až 600 diváků.

Stále usměvavý jubilant Rudolf Poláček. Foto archiv R.P.

V roce 1980 přišla nabídka dělat předsedu hokejového oddílu, tu však přebila jiná, tenisová. A tak se Poláček stěhoval na tři roky do německého Tirschenreuthu. A u tenisu už zůstal. Jako trenér nastoupil v roce 1984 do hotelu Golf, kde vydržel celých dvacet let. Během té doby se měl možnost potkat třeba s Jiřím Kodešem nebo s lady Luisou Abrahams.

Poté už si užíval jako rekreační tenista. Hrával často na kurtech u Lesního pramene nebo na Lokomotivě. S o čtyři desítky let mladším Petrem Jedličkou vyhrál v letech 2014 - 16 třikrát po sobě tenisový memoriál Petrova otce Václava. Což byl byvší výborný hráč fotbalu, také tenisový trenér a hlavně velký Poláčkův kamarád.

S přibývajícím věkem přestoupil Rudolf Poláček do kategorie sportovních fanoušků. Ve fotbalu fandí Bayernu München. A jen tak mimochodem: 23. června oslaví devadesátiny. Rudolfe, všechno nejlepší!

(Josef Milota)

[4] "Zdeněk Buchtele: S Richard Švandrlíkem jsme psali o všem, co se nám podařilo najít," Mariánskolázeňské Noviny (Mariánskolázeňské, Czech Republic), 22 červen 2018, ročník VI, strana 7.

The interview focuses on Buchtele's research interests and his lifelong work with Ing. Richard Švandrlík. Following is Marie Zahn's translation of the news article:

Zdeněk Buchtele: We wrote about everything we managed to find with Richard Švandrlík

The Mariánské Lázně newspaper and later news has been using articles and discoveries about the history of the local region by Zdeněk Buchtele. It is about time for people to get to know the personal [personality] of this always active local archeologist.

Have you been living in Velká Hleďsebe since your birth?

I was born in Mariánské Lázně but lived in Drmoul – school and army service, then after the service I lived in Mariánské Lázně and since the year 1980 in Hleďsebe.

What is your civil occupation?

It is the so-called black occupation. (Briefly I worked as a locksmith and then for the PBH as a plumber.) I also worked as a maintenance person in Potraviny Cheb and after the year 1990 as self-employed. From the year 2010 I am retired.

When did you get interested in the history of this region?

Did you get it through your genes? My mother was interested in history, though mainly in genealogies of Noble and Royal families. Maybe that was the base of my activity. I was more interested in the practical life of not only the nobilities, but also of simple people since the prehistoric times till the medieval time. Because there was quite a lack of information in this region, I became interested. Actively, after the year 1973 when I found several prehistoric ceramic pieces at the court Lískovec.

Did you have some system in monitoring of the region?

There are several important points. In the case of disappearing settlements, it is necessary to look for places where there is water. Where the paths used to go and where it was possible to farm even on small fields. There was a system in old indexes of settlements and communities. Individual places were always listed systematically in a certain direction. It was therefore possible to expect that, with a certain density of settlements in the past times there could be expected another discovery of a settlement in certain areas. Therefore, I do have a certain system, but often it is also good luck when my system can be used later. As long as I know you have inscribed everything carefully, measured and drawn.

What did you mainly pay attention to?

Yes, this is true. Sometimes drawing is more than a photo, especially if I can add measurements. I made a lot of plans, drawings of discovered things and objects. In the case of small monuments, it was practical, and often used by the police who used to take materials from me concerning lost objects, so that later they could evaluate them. I especially paid attention to damaged or destroyed things that I always felt sorry for. Often, I tried (sometimes unsuccessfully) to save them.

Who did you cooperate with? Did you have different roles?

There were many cooperators, but one was stable. Since 1974 we continually cooperated. It was Ing. Richard Švandrlík. He was an economist and I was the practical part. He spent more time in the archives. I was more often in the terrain. Then we wrote about everything we managed to find. Mutually we filled information in and edited the writings.

Did you cooperate with the Czechoslovak Academy of Science?

It was not a direct cooperation, but many publications that were published by the Academy [they] used and till now use the results of my investigations and published articles. After 1989 the department changed the name to Czech Archeological Society at Czech Academy of Science and I was a member until the year 2014.

With Mr. Švandrlík you published a lot of publications about the region. How many were there?

With my colleague Švandrlík we published about 25 publications and many articles, news, and information. From my own activities I can mention 7 books. All of them were about the history of this area around Mariánské Lázně.

I know that you have mapped well the Mariánské Lázně area and I also know that you tried to save the castle Valdštejn despite the fact that it did not have a happy end.

It did not have a happy end for our future activities, but it did have a happy end for the castle. The conservation work that we were doing back then for five years, saved the castle. Its destruction we averted, and the castle is standing until now, although unfortunately it is now in private hands, but it is accessible to people and open to public.

What was your most interesting finding or discovery?

As the most interesting finding I consider granite stone that was found under the hill. Its bottom part has the shape of a heart and upper part changes to the shape of an egg. Both shapes are separated from each other by dark vein. Heart and egg were always considered to be the symbols of life. In the upper part is evident a relief of Christ from sides surrounded by a mandorla, so called double hallow. In this decoration we could date this object to the year of 1000. Mandorla then appears only in paintings in the bases of chapel and churches.

Do you still continue with your expeditions?

I do, there is still enough to be discovered. I was only slowed down a bit by complete remake of exhibits in the museum in Mannský dvůr, where some of the individual objects were concentrated together to larger units. The exposition does not seem so chaotic now. Another slowdown is the age. Years multiply and a man cannot move so quickly as he used to. I still write about interesting matters. It would be a shame if they somehow get overlooked. At this moment I am working on the history of the village of Hamrník.

(Jana Drahokoupilová)[5]

---

[5] Marie Zahn, translator, "Zdeněk Buchtele: S Richard Švandrlíkem jsme psali o všem, co se nám podařilo najít," Mariánskolázeňské Noviny (Mariánskolázeňské, Czech Republic), 22 červen 2018, ročník VI, strana 7.

In 2021 Zdeněk Buchtele opened a second museum. His work is important to all local people who want to learn about the area's history and to all descendants of people from the Marienbad and Tepl areas. Selected books written by Buchtele and Ing. Richard Švandrlík are included at the end of this chapter.

Other local museums in today's western Czech Republic help build an understanding of the lives of those who immigrated to Calumet County. I have found these museums especially informative:

Local Museums in Western Bohemia

Tepl Monastery and Museum

Tepl Monastery was the estate owner of many of our ancestral villages during feudal times.[6] Tepl Monastery is being restored after its long demise during Soviet control, which lasted from 1968 until the 1989 Velvet Revolution. *Friends of Tepl* is an organization that has been helping with that restoration work since 1995. Members are from Germany, Czech Republic, Switzerland, Unit-

---

[6] František Palacký, *Popis Králowstwí českého, čili, Podrobné poznamenání wšech.* (1948), 402-403.

ed States and Chile. *Friends of Tepl* is dedicated to both the physical and spiritual reconstruction of the Tepl Monastery. Bringing people together on both sides of the border is important work to *Friends of Tepl.* More can be learned about their restoration efforts at https://www.freunde-stift-tepl.eu/.

Tours of Tepl Monastery are given in a variety of languages, including English. Visiting the museum is part of the monastery tour that tells visitors of its long history since 1193. The visitors' office sells postcards and pamphlets written in English about the monastery.

Tepl Monastery's old stable, used by the Soviets as barracks, is a hotel today. A restaurant offers lunch and dinner. The hotel would be convenient for researchers interested in using the monastery's library and in exploring area villages. Arrangements for the library's use must be made well ahead of time. The hotel website is https://hotelklastertepla.cz/.

Marienbad Town Museum

The Marienbad Town Museum is the oldest building in the historic part of Marienbad, built in 1818 as a spa hotel. The museum was founded in 1853 and has been in the renovated spa hotel since 1953.

Visitors can view a video in English explaining the historical background of the spa town and region. One room holds portraits of important guests of the spa hotel, including Johann Wolfgang von Goethe, Antonín Dvořák and King Edward VII. Exhibits in early medicine and spa treatments, mineral collections, and models depicting life in earlier times are all informative. The museum's website at https://www.marianskelazne.cz/en/tourist-attractions/town-museum/ includes pictures of selected exhibits.

Svaz Němců - region Chebsko z.s./Bund der Deutschen-Landschaft Egerland

This Homeland Museum is in the city of Cheb [Eger], about an hour's drive northwest of Marienbad. Exhibits include furniture and decorations of former German Bohemian families. Books are available for purchase. The museum offers German language classes to native Czech language speakers. The organization holds festivities and monthly meetings. It also publishes monthly newsletters with articles about current activities and events. More information is available on its website at https://www.egerlaender.cz/wir-ueber-uns.

Books Written in Czech about Ancestral Villages and their Residents

Zdeněk Buchtele and Richard Švandrlik have written many western Bohemian village histories, especially for villages in the Marienbad and Tepl areas. Each book begins with an early history of the village and surrounding area(s) up until the time of the book's publication. Village maps are detailed with house numbers and family names. Black and white and color photographs of the church, village houses, streets and people depict life in the village.

Selected books authored by Buchtele and Švandrlik describe the ancestral homes of some of the identified German Bohemians who immigrated to Calumet County, Wisconsin.

Buchtele, Zdeněk, and Richard Švandrlik. *Krajem Kolem Podhory*. Planá u Mariánských Lázni: K-Print, Tiskárna Kňourek, 2009.

The region around Podhory includes several villages located in the parish of Habakladrau:

The German place name for *Zádub* is *Hohendorf*. The family who emigrated from Hohendorf in 1882 is **Schusser.**

The German place name for *Závisín* is *Abaschin*. Families who emigrated from Abaschin beginning in 1855 are **Broeckel, Denk** and **Reinl**.

The German place name for *Milhostov* is *Müllestau*. Families who emigrated from Müllestau beginning in 1855 are **Huttl**, **Windirsch** and **Wurtinger**.

The book is 216 pages. Included are additional pages with color photographs.

Buchtele, Zdeněk, and Richard Švandrlik. *Mnichov městečko u Mariánských Lázni*. Planá u Mariánských Lázni: K-Print, Tiskárna Kňourek, 2010.

The German place name for *Mnichov* is *Einsiedl,* which is a village and parish. Families who emigrated from Einsiedl beginning in 1853 are **Christel, Groeschl, Loeb, Pimpl, Rudrich, Schurwon, Treml, Utschig, Zitterbart** and **Zucker**.

The book is 222 pages. Included are additional pages with color photographs.

Buchtele, Zdeněk, and Richard Švandrlik. *Ovesné Kladruby a zaniklé obce Vysočany a Výškovice*. Planá u Mariánských Lázni: Nakladatelství a vydavatelství Kňourek, 2012.

The German place name for *Ovesné Kladruby is Habakladrau,* which is a village and parish. Families who emigrated from Habakladrau beginning in 1855 are **Degl, Hammer, Hanika, Kogerer, Lodes, Neubauer, Pop, Rosner, Rott, Rummer, Schneider, Schusser, Steidl** and **Turba**.

Two other villages are featured:

The German place name for *Vysočany* is *Wischezahn*. Families who emigrated from Wischezahn beginning in 1856 are **Arbes, Lodes, Schmidt, Steiner** and **Zepnick**.

The German place name for *Výškovice* is *Wischkowitz*. The **Gintner, Nadler** and **Zepnick** families emigrated from Wischkowitz in 1856.

The book has 182 pages including pages with color photographs.

Buchtele, Zdeněk, and Richard Švandrlik. *Rájov Historie a památky*. Planá u Mariánských Lázni: K-Print, Tiskárna Kňourek, 2011.

The German place name for *Rájov is Royau,* which is a village and parish. Families who emigrated from Royau beginning in 1854 are **Cardinal**, **David**, **Egerer**, **Fischbach, Fischer, Hammer, Kutzer, Leitner, Lenz, Lodes, Miller, Nadler, Pimpl, Popp**, **Rahmer/ Rahma**, **Schreck**, **Schierl** and **Turba**.

The book is 120 pages with color photographs on front and back book covers.

Buchtele, Zdeněk, and Richard Švandrlik. *Sítiny Historie a Památky*. Planá u *Mariánských Lázni*: K-Print, Tiskárna Kňourek, 2011.

The German place name for *Sítiny* is *Rauschenbach,* which is a village located in the Einsiedl Parish. Families who emigrated from Rauschenbach beginning in 1854 are **David**, **Nadler**, **Niemochl**, **Schmidt** and **Wurtinger**.

The book is 111 pages with color photographs on the front and back book covers.

Buchtele, Zdeněk, and Richard Švandrlik. *Historie A Památky Obcí Vlkovice a Martinov* Planá u Mariánských Lázni: K-Print, *Tiskárna Kňourek, 2012.*

The German place name for *Vlkovice* is *Wilkowitz.* The village is in the Pistau Parish. Families who emigrated from Wilkowitz beginning in 1855 are **Schicker**, **Schmidt**, **Schmiedl** and **Schott**.

The German place name for *Martinov* is *Martinau.* The village is in the Pistau Parish. Families who emigrated from Martinau beginning in 1856 are **Hiederer** and **Pfroger**.

The book is 108 pages. Included are additional pages with color photographs.

Local Czech historians, museums and books are valuable for learning about villages and daily life of those who immigrated to Calumet County, Wisconsin. Equally important, perhaps, is learning about the lives of relatives who did not emigrate from the area. The history of western Bohemia just after World War II helps us understand the reason for continuing our research in Germany to find living relatives and information about ancestral families and villages in today's Czech Republic.

Chapter 10

German Resources: Research Associations, Homeland Museums and Books

Background

The end of World War II began the Expulsion of German-speaking people from areas in Czechoslovakia, parts of eastern Germany assigned to Poland, Hungary, Yugoslavia and Romania. The number of permanently displaced people from these areas is estimated at between 12 million and 14 million.[1] The German-speaking people living in the Tepl and Marienbad areas were no exception.

[1] R.M. Douglas, *Orderly and Humane: The Expulsion of the Germans after the Second World War* (New Haven: Yale University Press, 2012), 1.

On short notice, people were told to pack a small number of personal items before they were loaded onto trains and deposited amid the ruins of the Reich.[2] Fourteen trains exported thousands of German-speaking people from the Tepl-Petschau alone. Many expelled from this area were unloaded in Germany near Butzbach. All found themselves in need of food, water, shelter and a new place to call home.[3]

Today, the expelled Germans are known as the Sudeten Germans. Their new lives required them to work hard and to endure great trials. The Sudeten Germans organized themselves and decided to record the histories of their families, villages and homes as well as the personal memories of their beloved homeland. The Sudeten Germans have accomplished more than anyone could imagine.

Two German research organizations hold most of their work and offer repositories and publications to help Sudeten Germans and their descendants connect with their homeland and others expelled. The Sudeten Germans' work and research organizations are also essential for U.S. researchers whose ancestors emigrated from western Bohemia to Calumet County, Wisconsin.

---

[2] Douglas, *Orderly and Humane*, 1.

[3] Douglas, *Orderly and Humane*, 1.

German Research Organizations and Research Libraries

Arbeitsgemeinschaft Ostdeutscher Familienforscher e.V., (AGoFF)

AGoFF has more than 800 members worldwide. Their common interest is family history and regional history of historic German settlement areas in central and eastern Europe. AGoFF offers several publications and databases for its membership. Americans with ancestral ties to central and eastern Europe are welcome to join. Membership information in English is available on its website at https://agoff.de/.

Vereinigung Sudetendeutscher Familienforscher e.V., (VSFF)

VSFF promotes research in family and local history and heraldic fields relating to the historic regions of Bohemia, Moravia and Austrian Silesia. The association has resources both in paper and digital formats. The database is helpful in locating families and ancestral villages. Americans with ancestral ties to central and eastern Europe are welcome to join. Membership information is available on its website at https://www.sudetendeutsche-familienforscher.de/.

House of the German East or *Haus des Deutschen Ostens* (HDO)

The tasks and goals of the House of German East are found on its website at https://hdo.bayern.de/ueber/publikationen/index.php#:

> The House of German East (HDO) is a cultural, educational and meeting facility on the topics of the former German states and the German settlement areas in Eastern Europe The House of the German East organizes numerous cultural and educational events every year. In addition, it is the central funding agency of the Free State of Bavaria for cultural funding according to §96 BVFG. The house also has the largest public special library in Bavaria on the history and present of the German settlement areas in Central, Eastern and South-Eastern Europe.
>
> The House of the German East is a subsidiary authority of the Bavarian State Ministry for Family, Labor and Social Affairs.

HDO publishes a journal. Previous issues from 2004 are available online at its website. The address and contact information for the House of German East follows:

House of the German East, Am Lilienberg 5, 81669 Munich
Tel. 089/ 44 99 93 - 0
Fax 089/ 44 99 93 - 250

Email: poststelle(at)hdo.bayern.de

Bavarian State Archives

The Bavarian State Archives is in Munich. Government documents like charters, files and maps can be used in the reading room. Appointments are required for a visit.

Researchers are advised to begin with records kept by local authorities of a person's residence for the time after 1876. Researchers are advised to begin with registers for baptisms, marriages and deaths kept by ecclesiastic archives for the time before 1876.

Many online links are translated into English. Its website address is https://www.gda.bayern.de/die-staatlichen-archive-bayerns/. Inquiries can be made at the following address:

General Directorate of the Bavarian State Archives, Schönfeldstr. 5, 80539 Munich

Email: post officegda.bayern.de

Homeland Museums in Germany

The Sudeten Germans established Homeland Museums, mostly in Germany, to continue their work in sharing memories of family, villages and life as they and their ancestors had known it. Homeland Museums in Germany illuminate common ancestral bonds between immigrants from Calumet County, Wisconsin, and Sudeten Germans.

Sudetendeutschen Museum, Bad Neualbenreuth

Neualbenreuth Sudetendeutschen Museum for Marienbad District is in Bad Neualbenreuth, one of Germany's spa towns. One significant display shows two reconstructed model villages. Another important homeland display consists of 60 panels with each panel featuring a village from the Marienbad home district. Photographs, picture postcards and other historical information are included on each village panel.

The picture on the following page shows the museum's collection of village display panels:

One room displays a kitchen and/or living area complete with furniture, clothing, decorations and tools our ancestors would have

Foto 207: Broßer Bilderständer in den Grenzland-Heimatstuben in Neualbenreuth[4]

used. Another room is dedicated to religious statues and other religious objects our ancestors would have owned.

[4] Oswald Egerer and Karl Wach, *Kirchsprengel Habakladrau Mit den Orten Abaschin, Hohendorf, Müllestau, Wischezahn, Wischkowitz im Tepler Hochland.* (München, Germany: Erstauflage 1993-Neuauflage 2007) 288.

Marriage costumes with hats decorated with glass balls[5]

Tachauer Heimatmuseum in Weiden

Tachauer Heimatmuseum highlights the lives of German Bohemians who lived in the Tachau region before and during the Expulsion of Germans that followed World War II. The Tachau region is just south of Marienbad. Twenty-one trains expelled 25,000 people from the Tachau region from March to October

[5] Marriage costumes with hat decorated with glass balls Photograph. Digital image. Privately held by Joan Naomi Steiner, PhD [ADDRESS FOR PRIVATE USE,] Neenah, Wisconsin. 2018.

1946. More about the Expulsion for this region is found at https://www.tachau.de/d/museum/vertreibung/.

The museum tells the story of the Expulsion and people's lives before World War II. An ample collection of folk costumes and folk art illustrate their rich folk culture. The woman in the center of the picture on the previous page is a bride dressed in black, per the custom of the day. The women's hats are decorated with tiny glass balls made in their villages.

Mähring Musen

Mähring is a border crossing town and marketplace between Germany and the Czech Republic. The border crossing was especially important at the time of the Expulsion after World War II and the Velvet Revolution in 1989. An impressive photo documentation of the border reopening after the Velvet Revolution is featured in the museum, which is housed in the old school and town hall.

Models of "disappearing villages" and artifacts from the area show the character of this border town in earlier days. The picture on the following page is an example of models of farm buildings and life in the disappearing villages. The museum website is https://www.maehring.de/museen.

A model of a disappearing village[6]

Mähring Musen is one of twelve museums showcasing the lives of German Bohemians and their homeland villages. I recommend virtual visits to all 12 museums at the following website: https://daszwoelfer.de/de/das-zwoelfer.

[6] Disappearing villages. Photograph. Digital image. Privately held by Joan Naomi Steiner, PhD [ADDRESS FOR PRIVATE USE,] Neenah, Wisconsin, 2019.

Sudeten German Museum

The Sudetenland Museum opened October 2020 in Munich. English-language tours are available for a fee and must be requested online. The following description is from its website at https://www.sudetendeutsches-museum.de/:

> The Sudeten German Museum is the central museum for the German-speaking population in the Czech lands. Its permanent exhibition spans 1100 years of history, art and culture, presented in authentic objects from its collections, on an exhibition area of 1200 square meters.

The Sudenten German Museum is located at Hochstraße 10, 81669 Munich, Germany. Email the Museum at info @sudetendeutsches-museum.de.

Homeland Associations and Newsletters

Another valuable resource is the Sudeten Germans' Homeland Associations and newsletters organized by the Sudeten Germans. The newsletters feature ancestral villages and life before the Expulsion. Birthdays of living members are listed with home addresses. Special notices of those who have passed also are included. Meetings and festivities of the Homeland Association are highlighted. These associations offer both historical perspectives and current events in the lives of Sudeten Germans.

Homeland Association of Landschaft Egerland

The Czech and German names for the Homeland Association of Landschaft Egerland are Svaz Němců - region Chebsko z.s. and Bund der Deutschen - Landschaft Egerland, respectively. The contact person for their newsletter is Alois Rott at bgzeger@seznam.cz. Information about events and meetings can be found at http://www.egerlaender.cz.

Association for Plan-Weseritz

The German name for the Association of Plan-Weseritz is Heimatkreis Plan-Weseritz e.V. Current contact information for subscribing to the newsletter can be found at https://www.plan-weseritz.de/?Willkommen.

Homeland Association of Marienbad

The German name for the Homeland Association of Marienbad is Heimatverbandes der Marienbader Stadt und Land e.V. in der Sudentendeutschen Landsmannschaft, Sitz ub München. Contact information on how to subscribe is at plan-weseritz@tonline.de.

Franz Pany was chair of the Homeland Association of Marienbad from 1991 until his death in 2021. I visited him at his office in Munich, Germany, in February 2020.

Frau Dr. Steiner aus Wisconsin (USA) besuchte den Heimatverband

Zu einem kurzen Besuch beim Heimatverband der Marienbader kam Frau Dr. Steiner im Februar zum Vorsitzenden des Heimatverbandes.

Seit letztem Jahr versucht Frau Dr. Steiner die Geschichte ihrer Vorfahren und weiterer Bewohner aus Wischezahn/Habakladrau zu rekonstruieren.

Für Ihre Nachforschungen und zum Kennenlernen der Landsleute hat Frau Dr. Joan Naomi Steiner bereits letztes Jahr u.a. das Treffen auf dem Heiligenhof und das Pfarrfest in Pistau besucht. Auch dieses Jahr wird sie versuchen, den Kontakt zu pflegen.

Der Heimatverband wird die Arbeiten von Frau Dr. Steiner unterstützen.

Der Vorsitzende des Marienbader Heimatverbandes Franz Pany im Gespräch mit Frau Dr. Steiner aus den USA.

Wer den Heimatbrief liest, ist informiert!

Meeting with Franz Pany in Munich, Germany[7]

---

[7] "Frau Dr. Steiner aus Wisconsin (USA) besuchte den Heimatverband," Heimatverbandes der Marienbader Stadt und Land e.V. (March 2020): 86.

[Dr. Gert Reiprich arranged the meeting and to him I am deeply grateful.] I briefed Pany on the emigration research from the Tepl and Marienbad areas to Calumet County, Wisconsin, beginning in 1850. I also spoke about my research trips to the Homeland Reunion at the Heiligenhof in Bad Kissingen, Germany, in June 2019 and the Pistau Parish Festival in the Czech Republic in August 2019.

Pany wrote an article about our visit in the March 2020 issue of the *Heimatverbandes der Marienbader Stadt und Land e.V.* He stated that the Home Association supports research into immigration to Calumet County, Wisconsin. The article follows with a translation of Pany's message to the membership. Following is Michael Mautner's translation of the news article:

Dr. Steiner from Wisconsin (USA) visited the Homeland Association[8]

For a short visit to the Homeland Association of Marienbad Dr. Steiner came to the Homeland Association in February.

Since last year Dr. Steiner has been trying to reconstruct the history of her ancestors and other inhabitants from Wischezahn/Habakladrau.

[8] Michael Mautner, translator, "Frau Dr. Steiner aus Wisconsin (USA) besuchte den Heimatverband," Heimatverbandes der Marienbader Stadt und Land e.V. (March 2020): 86.

> For her research and to get to know the compatriots, Dr. Joan Naomi Steiner already visited last year, among others, the meeting at Heiligenhof and in Pistau. Also, this year she will try to maintain the contact.
>
> The Homeland Association will support the work of Dr. Steiner.

In summary, Sudeten Germans organized themselves and built memorials to their homeland through research organizations, museums, and Homeland Associations and newsletters. Their arduous work and dedication to preserve their homeland and family memories have given today's researchers bountiful resources for investigating immigrant families and ancestral villages.

Their work also paves the way for descendants of immigrants who settled Calumet County to locate descendants of those who did not emigrate from western Bohemia. Those living relatives are known today as the Sudeten Germans.

Books Written in German about Ancestral Villages and Their Residents

Egerer, Oswald, and Karl Wach. *Kirchsprengel Habakladrau Mit den Orten Abaschin, Hohendorf, Müllestau, Wischezahn, Wischkowitz im Tepler Hochland.* München, Germany: Erstauflage 1993-Neuauflage 2007.

Habakladrau Church Parish is made up of Habakladrau, Abaschin, Hohendorf, Müllestau, Wischezahn, and Wischkowitz villages. A brief history of each village is included. Each village map displays house numbers. Each house number lists residents going back to the early to mid-1600s in some cases. Also included are black and white photographs of residents, daily life, and village festivities.

Families who emigrated from Habakladrau beginning in 1855 are **Degl, Hammer, Hanika, Kogerer, Lodes, Neubauer, Pop, Rosner, Rott, Rummer, Schneider, Schusser, Steidl** and **Turba**.

Families who emigrated from Abaschin beginning in 1855 are **Broeckel, Denk** and **Reinl**.

The **Schusser** family emigrated from Hohendorf in 1882.

Families who emigrated from Müllestau beginning in 1855 are **Huttl**, **Windirsch** and **Wurtinger**.

Families who emigrated from Wischezahn beginning in 1856 are **Arbes**, **Lodes, Schmidt, Steiner** and **Zepnick**.

The **Gintner, Nadler** and **Zepnick** families emigrated from Wischkowitz in 1856.

The book is 297 pages.

Egerer, Oswald, Franz Hüttl, and Franz Pany, editors. *Kirchsprengel Pistau im Heimatkreis Marienbad: Geschichte und Chronologische Aufzeichnungen von den Orten: Pistau, Martnau, Hollowing, Untergramling, Kuttnau, Wilkowitz.* Bad Homburg v.d.H. und München, Germany: Heimatverband der Marienbader-Stadt und Land e.V. mit Sitz and Geschäftsstelle, circa 1990.

The Pistau Church Parish is made up of Pistau, Martnau, Hollowing, Untergramling, Kuttnau, and Wilkowitz villages. A brief history of each village is included. Each village is shown with a map displaying house numbers. Each house number lists residents, going back to the early to mid-1600s in some cases. Also included are black-and-white photographs of residents, daily life and village festivities.

Families who emigrated from Martanau beginning in 1856 are **Hiederer** and **Pfroger**.

Families who emigrated from Wilkowitz beginning in 1855 are **Schicker**, **Schmidt**, **Schmiedl** and **Schott**.

The book is 302 pages.

Familienbuchs [family books] provide essential information for researchers. Parish priests kept the parish family books. These books were not collected by the government because they were viewed as secondary sources to the vital records kept by the priest in official parish record books. However, several of these parish family books have survived and are important records, especially for emigration. The book details who lived in each house beginning as early as the 1600s and continuing until the Expulsion in 1945.

Information on house inheritance; family marriages with spouse names and their christening villages and house numbers; births of children; and deaths can be found. The priest also documented those who left for North America. Following are several parish family books that have survived:

Familienbuch Habakladrau Volume 1 Habakladrau, Wischezahn, Wischkowitz (Habakladrau, Cheb, Karlovarsky, Czech Republic). Families assembled by household, early 1600s–1940s). State District Archive, Cheb, Karlovarsky, Czech Republic.

> Families who emigrated from Habakladrau beginning 1855 are **Degl, Hammer, Hanika, Kogerer, Lodes, Neubauer, Pop, Rosner, Rott, Rummer, Schneider, Schusser, Steidl** and **Turba**.
>
> Families who emigrated from Wischezahn beginning 1856 are **Arbes, Lodes, Schmidt, Steiner** and **Zepnick**.
>
> The **Gintner, Nadler** and **Zepnick** families emigrated from Wischkowitz beginning 1856.
>
> The book is 282 pages.

Familienbuck Habakladrau Volume 2 Abaschin, Hohendorf, Müllestau (Habakladrau, Cheb, Karlovarsky, Czech Republic). Families assembled by household, early 1600s-1940s). State District Archive, Cheb, Karlovarsky, Czech Republic.

Families who emigrated from Abaschin beginning 1855 are **Broeckel, Denk** and **Reinl**.

The **Schusser** family emigrated from Hohendorf in 1882.

Families who emigrated from Müllestau beginning 1855 are **Huttl, Windirsch,** and **Wurtinger**.

The book is 334 pages.

Familienbuch *Einsiedl* (Einsiedl, Cheb, Karlovarsky, Czech Republic). Families assembled by household, 1700-1945. State District Archive, Cheb, Karlovarsky, Czech Republic.

Families who emigrated from Einsiedl beginning in 1853 are **Christl, Groeschl, Loeb, Pimpl, Rudrich, Schurwon, Treml, Utschig, Zitterbart** and **Zucker**.

The book is approximately 235 pages.

Familienbuch *Einsiedl des Dorfes Rauschenbach, Kschiha, Pfaffengrun, Passlas,* (Einsiedl, Cheb, Karlovarsky, Czech Republic). Families assembled by household, 1700-1945. State District Archive, Cheb, Karlovarsky, Czech Republic.

Families who emigrated from Rauschenbach beginning in 1854 are **David, Nadler, Niemochl, Schmidt** and **Wurtinger**.

Families who emigrated from Kschiha beginning in 1855 are **David, Egerer, Hammer, Leitner, Lenz, Neubauer, Pichl** and **Schmidt.**

The **Korn** family from Pfaffengrün emigrated in 1906.

The book is approximately 155 pages.

Familienbuch Pistau des Dorfes Martnau, Hollowing, Untergramling, Kuttnau, Wilkowitz, (Pistau, Cheb, Karlovarsky, Czech Republic). Families assembled by household, 1700-1945. Parish rectory. Held in München, Germany.

Families who emigrated from Martinau beginning in 1856 are **Hiederer** and **Pfroger**.

Families who emigrated from Wilkowitz beginning in 1855 are **Schicker**, **Schmidt**, **Schmiedl** and **Schott**.

The book is approximately 304 pages.

Familienbuch des Dorfes Royau (Royau, Cheb, Karlovarsky, Czech Republic). Families assembled by household, 1700-1945. Parish rectory. Held in München, Germany.

Families who emigrated from Royau beginning in 1854 are **Cardinal, David, Egerer, Fischbach, Fischer, Hammer, Kutzer, Leitner, Lenz, Lodes, Miller, Nadler, Pimpl, Popp, Rahmer/Rahma, Schreck, Schierl** and **Turba.**

The book is approximately 225 pages.

Giegold, Heinrich. *Tschechen und Deutsche Die Geschichte einer Nachbarschaft*. Hof, Germany: Frankenpost Verlag GmbH, 1993.

Czechs and Germans: The Story of a Neighborhood portrays the common history of common land between Czechs and Germans. The book is a compilation of a series of news articles published by Frankenpost-Verlag. The publishing house distributed the books as gifts to schools, government, libraries and state and local facilities of the region. Several Sudeten Germans whom I have met recommend reading this history.

The book is 88 pages.

Heinrich, Josef, editor. *Heimat-Chronik Müllestau.* Bad Windsheim, Germany: printed by Josef Heinrich, 1983.

The *Chronicle of Müllestau* contains many descriptions, photos, documentaries, and mood pictures of the village. The 1654 census lists landowners at that time. Several of the last German residents are featured with their pictures and reflections.

Families who emigrated from Müllestau beginning in 1855 are **Hüttl**, **Windrisch** and **Wurtinger**.

The book is 30 pages.

May, Josef Dr., Dr. Gert Reiprich, Inge Hubl, Rudolf Schweinitzer, Josef Eckert and Ernst Höhne, editors. *Heimatbuch Marienbad Stadt und Land Band I.* München, Germany: Heimatverband der Marienbader Stadt und Land e.V., 1977.

This book is essential for researching the Marienbad District. Volume I discusses the world health resort of Marienbad as well as its communities of the Marienbad District. Included is an extensive history of the resort area with its various hotels and cafes. Information about land, foliage and other interests in the area are extensively detailed. Maps with house numbers and biographies of former Marienbad residents and the surrounding communities are included.

The book is 696 pages.

May, Josef Dr., Dr. Gert Reiprich, Inge Hubl, Rudolf Schweinitzer, and Ernst Höhne, editors. *Heimatbuch Marienbad Stadt und Land Band II.*, München, Germany: Heimatverband der Marienbader Stadt und Land e.V., 1977.

Volume II features more than 50 villages in the Marienbad District. A brief history for each village is provided along with a map of houses with house numbers. Each house number lists residents going back to the years just before the Expulsion in 1945. Lists of World War I and II veterans are included for most villages. Residents who were expelled are listed along with their villages. Also included are black-and-white photographs of houses and residents.

The book is 1,215 pages.

Pany, Franz and Josef Lecher, editors. *Abaschin: Ein Gedenkbuch über einen Ort im Kreis Marienbad.* Munich, Germany: Heimatverband der Marienbader Stadt und Land e.V., 1986.

This book describes Abaschin, which is in the Marienbad District. Abaschin is featured with a brief history and map with house numbers. Each house number lists residents going back as far as the mid-1600s. Also included are black-and-white photographs of residents, daily life, and village festivities.

Families who emigrated from Abaschin beginning in 1855 are **Broeckel, Denk** and **Reinl**.

The book is 80 pages.

Pany, Franz and Dr. Gert Reiprich, editors. *Auschowitz Chronik des Ortes und Kirchsprengels 1273-1945 mit den Orten Flaschenhüette, Hammerhäuseln Hochofenhäuseln und Stanowitz.* Munich, Germany: Heimatverband der Marienbader Stadt und Land e.V., 1989.

This book features the villages of Auschowitz, Flaschenhüette, Hammerhäuseln, Hochofenhäuseln and Stanowitz. Each village is featured with an extensive history and map with house numbers. Each house number lists residents going back as far as the early to mid-1600s. Also included are black-and-white photographs of houses, residents, daily life and village festivities.

Families who emigrated from Auschowitz beginning in 1868 are **Eisen, Müller** and **Ries**.

The book is 106 pages.

Pany, Franz and Dr. Gert Reiprich, editors. *Royau Geschichte eines Pfarrodorfes im Kreis Marienbad.* Munich, Germany: Heimatverband der Marienbader Stadt und Land e.V., 1988.

The history of Royau village includes the parish history with black and white photographs of St. Peter and St. Paul Church. War Memorial pictures include the names of Royau veterans from World Wars I and II. A 1938 Royau map with house numbers lists each family in the village at that time. A list of Royau people who died after the Expulsion is listed by Royau house numbers. Each deceased person is listed with death dates and relocations after the Expulsion. This list is extremely helpful in locating living relatives and their descendants. The book is held at the Sudetendeutschen Museum Neualbenreuth in Bad Neualbenreuth, Germany.

Families who emigrated from this village beginning in 1854 are **Cardinal**, **David**, **Egerer**, **Fischbach**, **Fischer**, **Hammer**, **Kutzer**, **Leitner**, **Lenz**, **Lodes**, **Miller**, **Nadler**, **Pimpl**, **Popp**, **Rahmer/Rahma**, **Schreck**, **Schierl** and **Turba**.

The book is 59 pages.

Reiprich, Dr. Gert, editor. *Sudetendeutsche Familienforschung Yearbook 1973-1974*. Nürnberg, Germany: Noris Druck GmbH, 1974.

German Family Research is a family history collection for those families who originate from Sudetenland. Family histories written by researchers offer family ancestral lines and village historical perspectives.

The book is 99 pages.

Reiprich, Dr. Gert, editor. *Sudetendeutsche Familienforschung Jubiläumsband 1981*. Nürnberg, Germany: Vereinigung sudetendeutscher Familienforscher (VSFF), 1981.

Sudeten German Family Research is a family history collection for those families who originate from Sudetenland. Family histories written by researchers offer family ancestral lines and village historical perspectives. The publisher is Vereinigung sudetendeutscher Familienforscher (VSFF), which is discussed in the "German Research Organizations" section of this chapter.

The book is 368 pages.

Schmutzer, Josef, and Otto Zerlik, editors. *Das Tepler Land.* Geisenfeld (Hallertau): Heimatkreis Tepl-Petschau in der Sudetendeutschen Landsmannschaft, 1967.

This book is an essential documentation of the home circle of Tepl-Petschau in the Sudeten German spa triangle. Tepl Monastery, Tepl village and Marienbad are detailed with historic photographs. The 14 trains that exported German-speaking people from Tepl area are listed on page 389 along with departure dates. Chapter VII is more than 300 pages of Tepl district villages. Each village is featured with an extensive history and map with house numbers. Each house number lists residents going back to the time just before the Expulsion. Lists of World War I and II veterans are included for most villages. Also included are black-and-white photographs of houses, residents, and other historic buildings.

The book is 856 pages.

Newly Discovered German Language Resources for the Parishes of Royau and Grün

The parish of Grün is not in the Five-Parish Research Study. However, I am including these resources along with others being held in München, Germany. In some cases, the resources may offer additional information for the families of Royau and Einsiedl.

Examen sponsorum (actually 1745) 1786

The title translates as Examination of Sponsors (actually 1745) 1786. The book contains the bride examination book of the parish of Grün near Petscha (1745) 1786-1839.

The book is approximately 127 pages.

Examen sponsorum Localie Royau ab anno 1839

The title translates as Examination Sponsors by Royau Locale since 1839. The book contains bride examinations from 1839 to 1876.

The book is approximately 86 pages.

Firmungsbuch der Lokalie Royau vom Jahre 1840 (1892, 1905)

The title translates as Confirmation Book of the Royau Locale from 1840 (1892, 1905). The book contains a list of those who were confirmed from 1840-1943 with names of parents and godparents.

The book is approximately 98 pages.

Ordo Divinorum Localiae Royaviensis ab anno 1839

The title translates as the Order of the Divine Locales of Royau from the Year 1839. The book contains a diary of services on saints' festivals from 1839 to 1869.

The book is approximately 130 pages.

Militär Matrik Geistl. Vereinsbuch der (Lokalie) Pfarrei Royau vom Jahre 1840

The title translates as the Military Register, Spiritual Club Book of the (Locale) Parish of Royau from 1840. The book contains a list of members of the Spiritual Associations and Brotherhoods in the Locality/Parish Royau (1840) 1904. Additional associations include Christian Association of German Bohemia, Scapular Brotherhood, Rosary Association and Army of the Holy Cross.

The book is approximately 29 pages.

Provisionsbuch der Pfarrei Royau ab anno eccl. 1898

The title translates as the Commission Book of the Parish of Royau from 1898. The book contains a list of the sick who were provided services by the parish priest of Royau from 1898 to 1941.

The book is approximately 21 pages.

Sammlung der Stiftsbriefe bey der Localie-Kirche der heiligen Johannes und Paulus zu Royau

The title translates as the Collection of the Letters by the Local Church of the Saints John and Paul in Royau. The book contains mass donations to the church in Royau since 1828 created in 1919 by Pastor Stillip o. Praem.

The book is approximately 106 pages.

Verkündigungsbuch der Pfarrei Grün 1861

The title translates as Proclamation Book of the Parish of Grün 1861. The book contains the Sunday diary of the Pastor of Grün near Peschau from 1861 to 1867.

The book is approximately 195 pages.

Acknowledgements

I thank Dr. Gert Reiprich, who introduced me to valuable resources published by Sudeten German Homeland Associations. Dr. Reiprich also generously loaned me his privately held books. Without his guidance, this work could not have been accomplished.

I thank my cousin Rogene Steiner Kais, past president of the Milwaukee County Genealogical Society, for introducing me to Susan Chapman, Czech research chair. Susan's meticulous work on the immigration database and on sourcing data entries ensures the accuracy of the research. Any errors found are mine. I am grateful to Susan for many hours of inspiring conversation, especially during the challenging COVID-19 pandemic.

I am deeply grateful for the local and family historians of Calumet County who have come before me. How they accomplished their work without computers and the internet is utterly amazing! I especially want to thank Jeff Wettstein for sharing the work of Grandma Ottila S. Meyer Wettstein, who authored and co-authored dozens of Calumet County family histories. On her broad shoulders I stand with gratitude.

I thank Dr. Jack Schaffer for his research efforts in contributing to the One-Name Studies of Steiner and Denk in western Bohemia. He has tirelessly researched both the Denk and Steiner families, which has contributed greatly to the online database of German Bohemians.

I thank Mayor Aurelie Skřivanová, who escorted me around my homeland parish of Habakladrau/Ovesné Kladruby, Czech Republic. Mayor Aurelie's strong leadership is evidenced by the many improvements she has made in Habakladrau. Mayor Aurelie leads by example and is an inspiration to me.

I am grateful to the late local historian and author Zdeněk Buchtele. His work continues to inform and deepen my understanding of ancestral villages as well as the contemporary local history of the Marienbad and Tepl areas in the Czech Republic. I also am indebted to Buchtele for introducing me to local historian Dušan Benč of Tepl. I thank Dušan for the many hours he drove me around to see my disappearing ancestral villages. I am grateful for his willingness to share personal knowledge and love for the Tepl area through email exchanges. Petr Souček from Prague also generously shared resources that helped to verify my research.

I thank the American Center of the U.S. Embassy in Prague for hosting the 2020, 2021, and 2022 exhibitions of this immigration research. The exhibitions highlighted commonalities among the United States, especially Wisconsin, Germany, and the Czech Republic. A special thanks to Jaroslav Vítek for helping to coordinate these efforts.

I am indebted to Mike Dauplaise, president of M&B Global Solutions Inc., for his expertise in publishing and book design. A special thanks to Deb Anderson, Director of Archives and Area Research Center at the University of Wisconsin-Green Bay, for recommending Mike to me. I thank Jeff Ash for his tireless editing of the manuscript. I am also grateful to Andrea Schmid, First Chair of the Association of the Friends of Teplá Monastery (Verein der Freunde des Stifts Teplá) and its members for their ongoing support and encouragement.

I thank all whom I have met through this project and have gotten to know as friends and colleagues in Germany and the Czech Republic. A number of the Sudeten Germans are now documented cousins. I am grateful for their gifts of books, which have served as the foundation for this book. Their personal stories will forever live in my heart. My gratitude for their friendship cannot be put into words.

About the Author

Joan Naomi Steiner, PhD

Joan Naomi Steiner, PhD, was born and raised on her grandfather's farm in Calumet County, Wisconsin, and graduated from Chilton High School. She earned her doctorate from New York University and her Master of Science in Teaching English and Bachelor of Science degrees from the University of Wisconsin-Stevens Point.

Dr. Steiner's professional career includes teaching high school students for twenty-five years and administrating in school districts for seventeen years. She has also taught at the university level and worked as a consultant for more than forty school districts in Wisconsin.

While researching her paternal Steiner family history, Dr. Steiner uncovered a wave of immigration from villages of the Tepl/Teplá Monastery area in Western Bohemia to Calumet County, Wisconsin, beginning in the 1850s. She took five research trips to the Czech Republic and six trips to Germany during the course of her investigations.

Dr. Steiner's website is a database of findings and a repository for rare and invaluable sources from both Germany and the Czech Republic. You can find it at https://germanbohemianwisconsin.com/.

Made in the USA
Monee, IL
30 December 2023

50770875R00096